Sarah Hughes

SKATING TO THE STARS

Sarah Hughes

SKATING TO THE STARS

ALINA SIVORINOVSKY

B.
BERKLEY BOOKS, NEW YORK

ℝ

A Berkley Book
Published by The Berkley Publishing Group
A division of Penguin Putnam Inc.
375 Hudson Street
New York, New York 10014

PRINTING HISTORY
Berkley trade edition / December 2001

ISBN: 0-425-18464-1

Visit our website at
www.penguinputnam.com

Library of Congress Cataloging-in-Publication Data

Sivorinovsky, Alina.
    Sarah Hughes : skating to the stars / Alina Sivorinovsky.—Berkley trade ed.
        p. cm.
    ISBN 0-425-18464-1
    1. Hughes, Sarah, 1985- 2. Skaters—United States—Biography.
3. Women skaters—United States—Biography. I. Title.

GV850.H87 S58 2001
796.91'2'092—dc21
[B]
                                                                    2001043824

PRINTED IN THE UNITED STATES OF AMERICA

10   9   8   7   6   5   4   3   2

Waiting

March 2001
Vancouver, British Columbia

SARAH Elizabeth Hughes waited.

The fifteen-year-old figure skater from Great Neck, New York, stood behind the swinging door to the white oval barrier that surrounded the ice at the 2001 World Figure Skating Championship and waited to show off what she could do. She was so nervous and excited she hadn't slept a wink the night before. Her heart felt like it was jumping rope inside her chest, and her legs were kind of weak and rubbery, almost like someone had taken out her muscles and filled them with water, instead.

But Sarah wasn't too concerned. She figured she had a perfect right to feel this way. Because, when you got right down to it, this was it: the final night of the weeklong competition. The night of the event everyone had been waiting for, the night of the Ladies' Long Program, worth 50 percent of the total score. Tonight, the top twenty-four women in the competition (already whittled down from the original forty-seven who'd entered) would skate a four-minute program to the music of their choice. The skater whose jumps, spins, spirals, footwork and presentation the judges thought was the very, very best would be crowned the Ladies' Figure Skating World Champion for the year 2001.

Now, winning the World Championship in any old year could and should be considered a pretty big deal. But, this year, winning the title or even a medal meant even more than usual. Since March of 2001 was less than one year before the 2002 Winter Olympics, the medalists at the 2001 World Championships would be considered favorites to win medals at the upcoming Olympics, as well. It had been that way for many years. The 1991 World Champion, Kristi Yamaguchi of the United States, won the 1992 Olympics. The 1993 World Champion, Oksana Baiul from the Ukraine, won the 1994 Olympics. The 1997 World Champion, America's Tara Lipinski, won the 1998 Olympics. That was why the World Championship before the Olympics was an event everyone took extra seriously.

For Sarah, it felt as if everything was suddenly on a larger scale than it had ever been before. She could totally tell that the Olympics were only a year away now. Because she could also totally feel that key people like judges and other skaters and other coaches and even skating fans were starting to look at her much more closely. Suddenly, everyone was wondering: Should Sarah Hughes be considered one of the ones to watch at the Olympics?

Well, in a few minutes, they'd all find out.

In Vancouver, Sarah had already skated the long program she was waiting to perform now during an earlier qualifying round. In the qualifying round, with 20 percent of the overall score, she'd finished second behind the 1996, 1998 and 2000 World Champion, fellow American Michelle Kwan. In that round, the original forty-seven girls were cut down to thirty.

After the qualifying round, Sarah then skated a two-and-a-half minute short program (worth 30 percent of the score), where the girls were again cut down, this time to twenty-four. In the Short Program, Sarah finished fourth.

The standings now read:

Irina Slutskaya (Russia) 1st
Michelle Kwan (USA) 2nd
Angela Nikodinov (USA) 3rd
Sarah Hughes (USA) 4th

Sarah, as well as every single spectator in the arena, knew that a good skate, a "clean" skate, a skate with no mistakes might be enough to win her a medal. An incredible skate (and a mistake or two from the leader) might even be enough to win her the whole thing.

And so, bouncing up and down to keep her muscles from cooling off and cramping, Sarah Hughes waited.

She was dressed in a brand-new costume. It was designed to look like that of a Spanish Flamenco dancer. The dress sparkled with a red and black diamond pattern on the bodice, sheer sleeves that ended in ruffles at both elbows, and a dark, pleated skirt perfect for flaring up and twirling with every graceful spin. She wore no jewelry, except a pair of diamond stud earrings. (Skaters are advised to remove any jewelry before they step out onto the ice, so that a necklace or a bracelet doesn't get tangled up in their costume.) Her makeup was perfect. Dark eyeliner to accentuate her eyes, foundation, powder, and blush to even out her complexion and cover up any blotches or breakouts, and red lipstick to match her dress. To top it off, she wore a bright red silk flower behind her ear. It further accented the Spanish character of her program. Designer Tania Bass had made the costume (Sarah's third that year) especially for the skater, so that it would perfectly complement her choice of music, a selection from Ludwig Minkus's classic ballet, *Don Quixote.*

The music was a very familiar piece in the skating world. Great Britain's John Curry skated to it when he won the Olympics in 1976. European, World and Olympic Champion Viktor Petrenko used it for a few years during his competitive career. So did World and Olympic Champions Natalia Mishkotunik and Artur Dmtriev. Now it would be Sarah's turn to bring the great ballet to life on the ice.

But, for now, Sarah still waited.

In the meantime, all around her, everything was a blur. Standing by the barrier, waiting to be allowed onto the ice, Sarah could see the other skaters in her event. Because Sarah was skating in the final group of the night, a majority of the girls had already finished with their performances. Having changed out of their costumes and into warm-up clothes or sweats, they continued to hang around backstage. They looked kind of funny, dressed in normal clothes but still in full makeup, as they peeked out from behind the curtain that separated the skaters' entrance tunnel from the arena, and jumped up and down to get a better view over each other's heads of the competition.

But it wasn't just the other girls who were crowding around the area leading to the ice. Their coaches were there, too. The coaches were just as interested as the skaters in seeing how the competition went, how the other skaters performed, and how the judges marked and ranked all the performances.

Milling about next to the coaches were the volunteers. Most of them were local Canadians, sometimes skating fans, sometimes just good citizens who generously offered their time for free to insure that the entire event ran smoothly.

And next to the volunteers crowded the various television people. Skating is an extremely popular sport, not only in the United States and in Canada, but everywhere in the world. Television crews from almost every country in Europe and Asia had brought their cameras to document the event, and many of them were showing the Ladies' Final live. Sarah knew that as soon as she stepped onto the ice, dozens of video and still cameras would turn in her direction. They would shine their bright lights and click their flashes and point their microphones into her face.

And it would be Sarah's job to just go on with her business and pretend not to notice them.

Which wasn't very easy to do. There were so many of them!

To get one television show on the air, broadcast networks like ABC-TV in the United States or TF1 in France or NHK in Japan brought what looked like an army of producers and directors and camera people and researchers and announcers and production assistants. There were so many of them that they seemed to be everywhere. On the ice and off the ice, at the arena and in the hotel, backstage and right next to the barrier. All of them, it seemed, asked the same questions and all of them wanted the same thing. They wanted to photograph Sarah walking in, and they wanted to photograph Sarah stretching, and they wanted to photograph Sarah practicing and they wanted to talk, talk, talk at Sarah until she finally said what they thought they wanted to hear. But, in the end, it didn't matter to the TV people if Sarah stayed up and skated great or fell down and made a fool of herself in front of millions of people. Sarah was only a story to them, and, as someone who might possibly win the 2001 World Championship, Sarah would be the center of their attention as long as the competition went on.

Nevertheless, no matter how tough it may have been, while standing at the barrier Sarah did her best not to look at any of them. Instead, she looked straight ahead. She just looked at the ice, and she tried her hardest to shut out all the distractions and focus. Focus!

While Sarah waited, Irina Slutskaya from Russia was on the ice. In first place after the qualifying round and the Short Program, Irina was considered the one to beat at these championships. She'd had a terrific year, beating the defending World Champion Michelle Kwan every time they competed that season. Like Sarah, Irina was considered the athlete, while Michelle was considered the artist. Irina had two Triple-Jump-Triple-Jump combinations planned in her long program, making her program the most technically difficult one in the competition.

Now, as the clock ticked down Irina's four minutes on the ice, the Russian girl landed both of her combinations. They may not have been perfect, but they were landed. She didn't fall. Then, to top it all off, Irina even became the first woman to land a Triple-Jump-Triple-Jump-Double-Jump combo, as well.

Sarah waited. She waited through Irina taking her bows, and she waited through Irina getting off the ice, and she waited through Irina receiving her scores.

Finally, the announcer called out: "Representing the United States of America—Sarah Hughes!"

Sarah stepped out onto the ice.

She glided to the center.

She smiled confidently and saucily tossed her head to get into character. *Don Quixote* is the story of a young Spanish couple who, in the face of the girl's father refusing to let them marry, run away to be together. The boy then fakes a suicide to trick the father into giving them his blessing. Once the father does, the boy magically springs back to life, and the happy couple joyfully begin planning their wedding. At its heart and in its spirit, *Don Quixote* is a comical story, full of sly tricks and haughty attitude, all in the name of love.

When Sarah smiled and tossed her head, she was setting the scene and getting into the mood for her own performance. It was a gesture that every single one of the international cameras that had been tailing her all week recorded and transmitted back home.

Sarah's music began. The first, happy notes of *Don Quixote* floated across the filled-to-capacity arena.

"Pa-ra-pa-rum-pum-pum-pum-PUM-PUM!"

Sarah didn't move.

Again.

"Pa-ra-pa-rum-pum-pum-pum-PUM-PUM!"

Sarah still didn't move. Her coach, Robin Wagner, had choreographed the program for maximum drama. And nothing was more dramatic or tension-inducing for an eager spectator than sitting on the edge of your seat, wondering when the skater at center ice would finally launch into their program.

"Pa-ra-pa-rum-PUM!"

Finally, finally! She took her first step.

Finally, Sarah Hughes stopped waiting.

CHAPTER ONE

Family Matters

SARAH Hughes waited.

She waited for her turn to skate.

She was three years old.

Sarah's father, John Hughes, had been an ice hockey player. He played it growing up in Canada. He played it while attending Cornell University in the United States. He was so good he was the team captain when they won the U.S. College Championship in 1970. He was so good, he even thought about turning professional, attending a Maple Leafs' training camp after graduating from college. In fact, John Hughes loved hockey and skating so much that he built a tiny rink in the family's backyard for his kids to skate on.

Naturally, all of the Hughes' kids: Rebecca, David, Matthew and little Sarah, loved going outside to play on their homemade rink, even if, most of the time, there was more laughing and shrieking and snowball-throwing going on than actual skating. Especially for Sarah. In the beginning, she didn't so much glide gracefully across the ice as she just tagged along behind her brothers and sister, chasing them around the tiny rink.

But, as David and Matthew started taking after their dad and playing hockey, they needed a bigger ice rink on which to practice.

Their mom, Amy Hughes, began taking her talented brood to the Parkwood Ice Skating Rink in Great Neck, New York. The trip was only supposed to be for the older kids: Rebecca, then eight years old; David, then six; and Matthew, then four. But, three-year-old Sarah wanted to come, too.

In fact, if Sarah ever guessed that her mom was planning on going somewhere with the older kids and leaving Sarah with a sitter, she would hurry up and run to stand patiently by the door. Her mom would turn a corner with Rebecca, David, and Matt in tow, and there Sarah would be, ready and waiting for them, unwilling to be left behind. She'd even dress herself, putting on her very favorite piece of clothing in the whole world—her yellow snowsuit. And who could blame her for loving it? It was a terrific snowsuit, just perfect for a little girl as active as Sarah. It was so padded and thick that if she tripped and fell while running around the yard playing, she never got hurt. It was, without a doubt, the perfect thing to wear to an ice rink.

And it left Sarah's mother with no choice. If she wanted to make it to the rink on time, she would have to take Sarah, dressed up and looking like a roly-poly Twinkie, to the rink with the rest of the kids.

*

EVEN though it's not a World Championship arena, with bright lights and bustling television crews and thousands of cheering, clapping spectators, a local ice rink still features a lot of distractions for an energetic three-year-old like Sarah Hughes.

To start with, there's the skate rental counter. An area in the corner where casual skaters (kids and adults who skate a lot less than the Hughes') can tell the teenager on duty their shoe size, and be handed a pair of fitted skates from the dozens and dozens of different sets hanging on wall pegs, or lying in wooden cubbies.

And then there's the Zamboni. This machine, the size of a truck with huge wheels to match, stands by the side of the ice. As soon as a skating session is finished for the day, the Zamboni is used to scrape up the dirty, chopped up, leftover slush (like a tractor would pick up hay on a farm), and cover the ice with about an inch of water. The water then freezes and creates fresh clean ice for the next round of kids to skate on. (Not only three-year-olds like watching Zambonis. At big competitions and skating shows, the audience often gives the Zamboni driver a big round of applause as he skids off the ice.)

Of course almost as interesting as the rental counter covered in skates and the roaring Zamboni, are the big swinging doors that lead to the ice. And then there are the Formica tables and padded benches to climb on. And, of course, the candy and hot chocolate machine.

Amy Hughes didn't want Sarah getting distracted and running off while her mother was busy taking care of the older children. So, thinking she was being practical, Amy sat all of her kids in a line on one of the rink benches, and, because they were too young to do it themselves, began helping them tie up their skates.

Starting with the littlest skater, Sarah.

At the time, Amy didn't realize she was making a mistake.

As soon as Sarah's skates were tied, the three-year-old dynamo jumped off the bench, and ran at full speed toward the rink. She was through the heavy swinging doors and out on the ice before her mother, who was pregnant with Sarah's little-sister-to-be Emily and couldn't move as fast as she'd like to, even had time to straighten up.

Worried that Sarah would hurt herself all alone out on the ice, her mother ran as far as the rink's barrier. She called Sarah's name, but, her daughter was having too much fun to listen, or she pretended that she couldn't hear. Finally, Amy had to call over an ice-monitor, one of the teenage boys hired by the rink to skate around and see that the skaters didn't get into any trouble, and ask him to fetch Sarah.

"Her. Yes, her." Amy pointed. "The little girl in the yellow snowsuit."

THE next time the Hughes family went skating, Sarah's mother thought she had a plan for making sure Sarah didn't escape again.

Just like the last time, she lined up all of her children on the rink's bench. Only, this time, she decided to tie Sarah's skates last.

After all, Sarah couldn't run off if her feet were flopping around inside a pair of untied boots, could she?

It was a good plan. Except the only problem was, Sarah really, really, really wanted to get on the ice. And, frankly, this sitting around, waiting to have her skates tied just wasn't going to work. Sarah didn't want to be the last one out there!

So Sarah sat there, in her yellow snowsuit, and she tried to think her way out of this very pressing problem. She looked at her mother, tying Matt's skates. Then she looked down at her own untied boots. It didn't look so hard, this tying your shoes business. Sarah had seen her mother do it a thousand times before, and it always appeared really easy when she did it.

Cautiously, Sarah lifted her foot, so she could get a closer look at the untied boot. The skate's padded tongue looked back at her, kind of squinting behind the loose, white laces. Gingerly, Sarah pinched one of the laces between her thumb and her finger, and pulled, just like she'd seen her mother do. She felt a slight tightening around her foot.

This was good.

This seemed to be a step in the right direction.

Emboldened, Sarah pulled on the other lace. More tightening. Good, good, she really had the hang of this, now. She took the two laces with both hands, and pulled really hard. Tah-dah! There. Done. All nice and tight.

Except that now she still had to figure out how to tie them.

Sarah's fingers were pretty small, and, now that she was really thinking about it, that over and under and loop-the-loop stuff did seem a little harder than it had just a few seconds ago. Not to mention that it didn't look like there was much lace left up on top to fix into a bow like her mother always did. Maybe Sarah should just sit quietly and wait her turn. Mom would get to her eventually.

But, waiting was so hard!

And sitting, well, sitting really wasn't nearly as much fun as skating.

No, Sarah decided, this was something she'd have to learn to do for herself. And the sooner the better. Like, right now.

And so, even though she was just three years old and she'd never ever in her life tied a shoe, much less a skate, Sarah bent over and she thought as hard as she absolutely, positively could.

Now that she's almost grown up, Sarah doesn't remember exactly how she figured it out. All she knows is, before her mother or any of the other kids knew it, little Sarah stubbornly and determinedly had taught herself how to lace up her own skates.

And, just like last time, she ran out through the swinging doors. Toward the ice.

✳
 ✳
✳ OF course, once she mastered the art of tying, there really was no stopping Sarah Hughes. At age four, she began taking regular lessons at the same ice rink where she'd first learned to lace up her skates. By only age six, she was so good she was performing in Lake Placid, New York, alongside 1992 Olympic Champion Kristi Yamaguchi.

Skating in a show is very different from skating in your home rink, or at a competition. In a regular rink or even at a qualifying or world-class competition, the lights are always on. Skaters can see where they're going and they can see the people in the stands. At a show, though, the lights are out. Skaters perform under a bright spotlight moving across the dark ice, which makes it much harder to see where the rink's barriers are, and almost impossible to see someone in the audience.

Most six-year-olds might have been intimidated. They might have gotten scared when they couldn't see their parents, or when they had to step on the ice right next to a National, Olympic and World Champion.

But not Sarah.

For Sarah, it was all just business as usual. And it was great experience for when, a few years later, she and her younger sister, Emily, both performed at the opening of New York City's most famous outdoor ice rink, Rockefeller Center, at the invitation of the center's director, two-time World Bronze Medalist JoJo Starbuck.

International Figure Skating Magazine's Editor-in-Chief Lois Elfman remembers, "They were very cute, but, they were very good, too."

Even though Sarah and Emily hadn't won any serious medals yet or even competed at any major competitions, the Hughes girls quickly became well known around the New York area as the best ones to invite to perform in your skating exhibitions. TV star Kathie Lee Gifford even had Sarah and Emily on one of her Christmas specials.

Then, when she was eight years old, Sarah was invited by Russian coach Natalia Dubova to do a tour of France and Europe alongside World Ice Dance Champions Maia Usova and Alexandr Zhulin and European Champion Surya Bonaly.

Since she was so young, Sarah doesn't remember too much about the tour or about Europe, but she does remember seeing the Eiffel Tower.

Sarah's dad, on the other hand, has very clear memories of his young daughter's shining moments.

John Hughes told *U.S. Figure Skating Online*, "I was sitting there, watching Sarah in the spotlight. All of the people around me had paid a lot of money to see this, and there's my daughter down there on the ice! Sarah didn't let anything get to her. That's when I felt this was something she was going to do."

SERIOUS skating requires very serious dedication from the boy or girl who decides to pursue it.

Anyone can just go to an ice rink to skate a public

session in the middle of the afternoon. But serious skaters practice jumps and spins that could be downright dangerous if they tried to do them around people who don't know enough about the sport or can't skate fast enough to get out of the way.

That's why competitive skaters need to get private ice time. They need to skate at a time when only other serious skaters are on the ice, and not too many of them, at that. Single skaters like Sarah usually have their own practice ice, pair skaters have their own time, and ice-dancers their own. That way, nobody gets hurt.

But, with so many skaters wanting private ice (and that's not even counting the hockey players who don't want to practice with any figure skaters around), ice rinks often have to schedule these sessions at very uncomfortable hours—like early (5 A.M.) in the morning!

About having to get up so early, day after day, week after week, year after year, Sarah told *The Today Show*'s Katie Couric, "It's really difficult. Some days you're like— Ugh, I just want to stay in bed all day." (No wonder then, that when asked what her greatest achievement was, Sarah listed getting out of bed in the morning right at the top!)

To make matters worse for Sarah, the rink where she skates now isn't anywhere near her house. She has to get up even earlier than some other skaters, because it takes her forty-five minutes of driving time to make it to the rink. If she's really honest, instead of just being polite, Sarah admits that she doesn't like to drive to the rink and back, because it limits her all-important time to herself. But, she realizes it's a part of her life, the life that she's chosen for herself, and she does her best to deal with it gracefully.

When faced with such a difficult situation and long, lousy commute, many skaters make the choice to move away from home so they can be closer to their ice rink.

1993 U.S. Silver Medalist Lisa Ervin was eight years old when she left her mom and dad behind to move to Cleveland and train with the 1960 Olympic Champion Carol Heiss Jenkins. 1996 World Champion Todd Eldredge was ten when he began following his coach Richard Callaghan all around the country. 2001 World Champion from Russia Evgeny Plushenko was twelve when he moved from his home in Siberia to St. Petersburg.

Two-time U.S. Men's Champion Scott Davis. Great Britain's 1980 Olympic Gold Medalist Robin Cousins. 1989 World Champion from Japan Midori Ito. 1990 World Champion Jill Trenary. 1995 World Champion from China Lu Chen. 1989 World Junior Champion Jessica Mills. The list of skaters who left home at a young age to pursue their dreams goes on and on and on.

And, even in cases where the traveling child took one parent with them, the arrangement still meant a long separation from their other parent, not to mention their brothers and sisters.

1998 Olympic Champion Tara Lipinski lived in apartments all over the country, including Newark, Delaware, and Detroit, Michigan, with her mother, while her dad remained back home in Texas. 1996 U.S. Junior Champion and Pairs World Competitor Shelby Lyons lived in a Col-

orado Springs apartment with her mom while Dad stayed
home in Oswego, New York.

1968 Olympic Champion Peggy Fleming. 1976 Olympic
Champion Dorothy Hamill. Sisters Michelle and Karen
Kwan. 1998 U.S. Dance Champion Jamie Silverstein. Again,
the list of families separated by skating goes on and on.

But, despite proof that leaving home could lead to a
successful skating career, Sarah Hughes doesn't want to be
separated from her family. Mainly because they're her most
important support system.

Sarah's coach, Robin Wagner, agrees with Sarah's decision, and praises Amy and John Hughes for managing to
be supportive without being overbearing, a very rare thing
in skating. It's more common to find parents who want to
be super-involved in every aspect of their skaters' lives.
They come with them to the rink every day, they phone
the coach every night, and they make all the decisions and
call all of the shots. Some, like European Champion and
three-time World Silver Medalist Surya Bonaly's mom have
even gone so far as to fire their child's professional coach
(in the middle of a competition!) and announce that
they'd be the ones coaching them from now on.

But, Sarah's parents and her coach have a very open
and excellent relationship regarding decisions about
Sarah's career, things like where they want her to go and
how they want her to go there. Everyone agrees that such
good communication and atmosphere has certainly con-
tributed to a very stable environment.

Besides, with six kids, Sarah's parents simply don't have

the time to be overly involved in her life and career. For one thing, Sarah's not the only skater in the family, there's also little sister Emily. And for another, all of the kids are very busy, and have their own extracurricular interests. Matt and David play hockey, Taylor takes acting classes.

So, to make this busy and active family work, everyone has to pitch in—there's no room for star trips or prima donna attitudes. The Hughes' are one large family who know how to pull together. And that includes all the generations!

Since both of Sarah's parents work, Sarah's grandparents often help out. Her father's mom used to come and stay with the Hugheses for months at a time whenever Sarah's mom had a new baby. In addition, it's up to the older kids to look out for the younger ones. For instance, Sarah's older brother Matt knows that when he comes home from school, he can't go out and do his own thing until he's picked up the baby of the family, Taylor, and taken her wherever she needs to go. Even Sarah, the busiest one, has to do her share of baby-sitting duty. Before she left for the 2001 World Championships, Sarah baby-sat for Taylor and two of her friends. The quartet hung out, made waffles, and just basically had a good, normal, non-skating time.

It's those kind of fun family experiences that Sarah knows she'll miss if she leaves home to train at a big skating center. And it's something she simply refuses to do. It's not worth it. Skating isn't worth giving up your whole life for. Sarah would rather know that, even if she doesn't make it in skating, she can still say that she gave it her best shot, and, as she explained to *The Daily News*, "I'll have been around my family."

That's what really matters.

CHAPTER TWO

Ladies' Skating: The Early Years

If Sarah Hughes wins a medal at the 2002 Winter Olympics in Salt Lake City, Utah she will become a part of a long and illustrious tradition of women skaters.

The first woman to win a medal on the international level in figure skating was Great Britain's Madge Syers. She came in second at the 1902 World Figure Skating Championships—in the Men's Event!

What happened was simply this: It had never occurred to the organizers of the World Figure Skating Championship that a woman might want to enter their highly athletic contest. The organizers had simply assumed that all of the entrants would be men, as had been the case since the Championship was first launched in 1896.

However, exactly one hundred years before the 2002

Olympics, Madge Syers not only applied to compete, she nearly won the whole thing.

Of course, immediately after that almost happened, the International Skating Union's (ISU) Congress decided that, oh, no, this wouldn't do at all! From now on, women would be forbidden from competing at an international men's championship. So, like Sarah, Madge Syers was forced to wait. She was forced to wait for four years, before the ISU gave in and created a women's championship to run concurrent with the men's. Once that happened, though, Madge promptly won the 1906 and the 1907 Women's World Championship, and the 1908 Olympic gold medal.

Following Madge's example, a host of great ladies' champions came after her. Skaters from Hungary won the World Championship seven years in a row. And, after a break of seven years due to the outbreak of World War I, Austria came onto the scene as Herma Plank-Szabo won five back-to-back Championships.

However, it was a little girl from Norway named Sonja Henie, who really captured the imagination of the world with her skating.

At the 1924 Olympic Games in Chamonix, France, eleven-year-old Sonja Henie was the youngest competitor (just like thirteen-year-old Sarah Hughes was the youngest competitor at the 1999 World Figure Skating Championships). She was cute, and she was energetic, but, in spite of all that, Sonja finished dead last at her first Olympics.

Four years later, though, it was a different story altogether. Fifteen-year-old Sonja Henie won the first of her three Olympic Gold medals, and, along the way, she revolutionized skating, as well.

Sonja shortened her skirts to above the knee, added daring jumps and spins to her program, and performed with such personality that she not only became a skating star, she also became a bona-fide movie star.

After her Olympic triumphs, Sonja moved to Hollywood and starred in movies like *Thin Ice* (1937), *Sun Valley Serenade* (1941), and *Wintertime* (1943). At one point, she was the biggest box-office draw in the country.

After Sonja, Canada's Barbara Ann Scott won the 1948 Olympic Gold and the hearts of the world. She was followed by America's Tenley Albright, a silver medalist at the 1952 Olympics and a gold medalist in 1956. However, unlike Sonja and many past champions, Tenley never had the world stage all to herself. For most of Tenley's reign, there was another American wonder waiting in the wings.

She was a tiny sprite named Carol Heiss, and, like Sarah Hughes, Carol was only thirteen years old at her very first World Championship in 1953.

She recalls, "I weighed all of sixty-seven pounds, and I think I was about four-foot-seven. But, I was the national junior champion, and I was so excited to be a member of the team. I had no record before the World Championship. Nobody had any idea how I was going to do. And I wanted to say, you know, I have just as much right to be here as anyone else. I've made the team. I came in fourth that year, so I ended up being the number two girl. I remember, the next morning, saying to my coach, 'Do you realize I'm the fourth best lady in the whole world?' And she said, 'That's nice. But, don't say that to anyone else.' She wanted to make sure I didn't come off being a little conceited."

As a result of her own experience, Carol doesn't think there is such a thing as being too young for the World Championship.

"I think if they can do the job, then why not? I think anyone who comes out of the U.S. Nationals to make the World team has what it takes, because it's so difficult to get out of our country."

Seven years after attending her first World Championship, Carol Heiss won the Gold medal at the 1960 Olympics, held in Squaw Valley, California. Afterward, Carol turned professional, marrying the 1956 Men's Olympic Gold Medalist, Hayes Allen Jenkins. She also tried for a movie career of her own with the film *Snow White and the Three Stooges*.

It was a strange combination, skating and the Three Stooges. The movie wasn't a great success.

After Carol, came Peggy Fleming, the Olympic Champion in 1968. With the advent of color television, the soft-spoken California teenager skated into the public's hearts by way of their living rooms.

And after Peggy, it was Janet Lynn. Though she only won the bronze medal at the 1972 Olympics in Sapporo, Japan, she forever endeared herself to the public when, after falling on a spin, Janet gracefully got up—still smiling.

Dorothy Hamill won the 1976 Olympics, and went on to headline various television specials and skating shows. Her short and sassy haircut became a favorite with girls all across the country.

Unlike Peggy, who'd been considered an artist on the ice, Dorothy was deemed more of a jumper. While Peggy only need a double axel to win the Olympics, by the late 1970s, triple jumps were becoming more and more important to the sport. 1977 and 1979 World Champion Linda Fratianne made them regular staples in her programs, and Elaine Zayak landed a then record seven triple jumps to win the 1982 World Championship. By the time Elaine and Rosalynn Sumners were duking it out for the U.S. title in the early 1980s, women were doing almost all of the difficult triples, except for the triple axel. Japan's Midori Ito had even landed a triple toe loop-triple toe loop combination at the 1981 World Junior Championships.

Naturally, a new breed of skating called for a new breed of skater. Which was why, by the 1990s, it was time for the jumping beans to take center stage. Jumping beans like Sarah Hughes.

CHAPTER THREE

Expectations

SARAH Hughes may have taught herself to tie her own laces and boots. But, realistically, she couldn't very well teach herself to become a champion ice skater.

Enter Robin Wagner.

Like her star pupil, coach Robin Wagner is also rather unusual for a world-class, championship trainer.

For one thing, although she was a skater, Robin was never a champion. She qualified for and competed at the 1974 and 1975 U.S. National Championships, but left without a medal. In high level skating, it's more typical for the coaches of champions to have once been champions themselves.

Tamara Moskvina, Russian coach of Olympic Pair Champions Oksana Kazakova and Artur Dmtriev and World Pair Champions Elena Bereznaia and Anton Sikharulidze won a World Silver medal herself in Pair Skating. Her partner back then was Alexei Mishin, who went on to coach 1994 Olympic Champion Alexei Urmanov and 2001 World Champion Evgeny Plushenko.

1980 Olympic Ice Dance Champions Natalia Linichuk and Gennady Karpanosov coached Olympic Champions Oksana "Pasha" Grishuk and Evgeny Platov. 1960 Olympic Champion Carol Heiss Jenkins coached star Americans like Timothy Goebel and Tonia Kwiatkowski.

And even in cases of coaches who weren't champions themselves, the ones who are known for producing World and Olympic medalists tend to be "big names." They are coaches famous for producing almost an assembly line of winners.

"Big name" coaches like the late Carlo Fassi, who trained 1968 Olympic Champion Peggy Fleming, 1976 Olympic Champions John Curry and Dorothy Hamill, 1980 Olympic Champion Robin Cousins and 1990 World Champion Jill Trenary.

Like Richard Callaghan, who coached 1996 World Champion Todd Eldredge, 1998 Olympic Champion Tara Lipinski, and, for a while, Angela Nikodinov, one of Sarah's main American competitors.

Like John Nicks, who coached World Bronze Medalists JoJo Starbuck and Ken Shelley, 1979 World Pair Champions Tai Babilonia and Randy Gardner, and now coaches two of Sarah's biggest competitors, 1999 U.S. Silver Medalist Naomi Nari Nam, and 2000 U.S. Silver Medalist Sasha Cohen.

And, of course, like Frank Carroll, who coached 1977 World Champion Linda Fratianne, two-time World Bronze Medalist Tiffany Chin, U.S. Champion Christopher Bowman, and the woman to beat in Salt Lake City, four-time World Champion Michelle Kwan.

Before Sarah Hughes, Robin Wagner had never coached a student to the World Championships.

The situation has its drawbacks, of course. Robin doesn't have the experience of a Callaghan or a Carroll. She doesn't know as many tricks for getting her skater noticed, and she doesn't know as many people for playing political games. But, there are also advantages to being a less well-known coach's top student.

When a coach has too many champions in their stable, a skater can start to feel ignored. 1984 Olympic Champion Scott Hamilton left "champion maker" Carlo Fassi for Don Laws, because he wanted to be his coach's top priority. World Champion Alexei Yagudin left Alexei Mishin for the same reason.

But, both Scott and Alexei switched over to coaches who at least had a proven record of training winners in the past.

Robin Wagner had no such record.

And yet, even though it's been suggested to her, Sarah refuses to leave Robin in the same way as she refuses to leave her family.

The way Sarah sees it, there are three things she can't live without. Her family. Her skating. And her coach.

Her parents back up Sarah's decision. Her father maintains that there is no need for Sarah to leave Robin and switch over to a big name coach who, some whisper, will be better equipped to take her to the top. As far as John Hughes is concerned, Sarah has the best of all worlds living at home and training with Robin. It works for her.

That's because, to Sarah, Robin is more than just a coach.

To begin with, they spend an unusually large amount of time together.

Six mornings a week, Sarah's mother drives her daughter to the parking lot of the local Macy's store in Manhasset. There, Robin picks Sarah up, and they begin their commute from Long Island to Hackensack, New Jersey, to practice at the Bergen County rink.

It's not the closest ice arena, but its four ice surfaces and a wonderful ballet room for off-ice work make the long, daily drive worth it for both Robin and Sarah.

To some people it might seem strange, Sarah's parents allowing their young daughter to spend hours upon hours under the influence of someone who might, under different circumstances, be considered a total stranger. But, Sarah's parents are happy with the arrangement. They trust Robin completely when it comes to Sarah and her skating. Robin is in charge of coaching, and Sarah's parents don't want to interfere at all. All the skating decisions are Robin's. And besides her being a terrific coach, the Hughes think she's a terrific person.

Sarah's mom believes they are very lucky to have Robin, especially since she also lives nearby. Amy thinks Robin has been a wonderful coach and role model. She's well read, she's intelligent, she's a college graduate (Barnard College in New York City) and she's provided a lot to Sarah's growth. Besides, after everything is said and done, student and coach have a great time together.

On a good day, Sarah and Robin's drive to New Jersey takes forty-five minutes. On a bad day, it can take an hour and a half. Some days, Sarah and Robin spend up to three hours together in the car. They have to cross two bridges, and traffic can frequently stall. To pass the time, Sarah and Robin often listen to their favorite CDs (Sarah loves Celine Dion, Britney Spears, Christina Aguilera, Ricky Martin and almost all of the boy bands), work on Sarah's homework, or just talk about anything and everything that pops into their heads.

Sarah believes it's important for her to have Robin in her life. She feels like she can talk to her coach. Robin helps her with both her skating and her feelings. Sarah believes if you can't trust your coach, it's only you against the whole world.

And nobody wants to live feeling like that.

"A coach has to know what the skater is thinking and feeling every moment," Robin told USFSA.org. "I never want it to be the kind of relationship where I say 'Just listen to me.' We have a lot of down time together and spend a lot of time on the road. It's nice to have the ability to laugh and play here and there. But, (Sarah) knows me, and when we're at the rink, it's business and I'm the coach. It's very easy for us to shift into the coach/student mode, which makes it easy to coach her. She's very eager to learn. Sarah knows our relationship changes when we arrive at the Ice House in Hackensack. But she's got to know I'm with her at heart."

✳
  ✳

✳ ROBIN Wagner began working with Sarah in 1995. She started off as simply her choreographer, then eventually moved into the full-time coaching role.

From the beginning, the tiny nine-year-old had, according to Robin, fantastic athletic ability. She was an excellent jumper, and, by 1995, being a jumping bean was the key thing in skating.

Progress came briskly and logically. Robin remembers that learning the double axel took over two years and was a landmark for Sarah. After that, all of her triples came pretty quickly.

But, in addition to her jumping, Robin also noticed that Sarah had a delicate presence on the ice. The combination worked for Michelle Kwan. Robin thought it could and would work for Sarah Hughes, too.

Although, naturally, nine-year-old Sarah wasn't ready to take on the world quite yet.

For one thing, when people talk about champion figure skaters, they are usually talking about skaters at the "Senior" level. Senior level skaters are the ones who go to the World Championships and the Olympics.

In skating, there are seven levels, as set by the United States Figure Skating Association (USFSA). Those levels are: Preliminary, Pre-Juvenile, Juvenile, Intermediate, Novice, Junior, and Senior.

To move up from one level to the next, aspiring skaters need to take tests in front of a panel of judges. Each judge gives the skater a number score, like the ones seen on television after a performance, but they also mark them either "Pass" or "Retry." Once a skater has received a "Pass," they can compete at the next level.

In 1995, Sarah Hughes was a Novice-level skater.

That meant she could finally start the long road that leads to qualifying to compete at United States National Championships. (Novice-, Junior-, and Senior-level skaters compete at the same Nationals, although, of course, in different divisions. Juvenile and Intermediate skaters have a Nationals of their own, and Preliminary skaters only compete locally.)

Now, competing at the Nationals isn't just a matter of showing up and announcing, "I'm here! Let me skate!"

Every skater at Nationals has earned their spot through participating in a qualifying competition.

There are two key qualifying competitions to make it to Nationals. A regional competition, called the Regionals, and a sectional competition called the Sectionals.

As of 2001, the United States is divided into nine regions: North Atlantic, Southern Atlantic, New England, Northwest, Midwest, Southwest, Northern Pacific, Central Pacific, and Southern Pacific. It is also divided into three Sections: Easterns, Midwesterns, and Pacific Coasts.

The top four skaters in each division from the North

Atlantic, South Atlantic, and New England regions earn the right to compete at Easterns. The top four skaters in each division from the Northwest, Midwest, and Southwest regions earn the right to compete at Midwesterns. The top four skaters in each division from the Northern Pacific, the Central Pacific, and the Southern Pacific regions earn the right to compete at Pacific Coasts.

Afterward, the top four skaters in each division at Eastern, Midwesterns, and Pacific Coasts are the ones who qualify for the Nationals on the Novice, Junior and Senior level.

Sarah's first major qualifying competition with Robin was the 1996 North Atlantic Regional Novice Championship.

She was ten years old.

A Regional competition is nothing like a World or even a National event.

Instead of a big arena with lights and cameras and thousands of people in the stands, a typical regional competition is usually held at a local rink not too different from the sort of rink skaters practice in every day.

The dressing rooms are small and cramped. Some girls even have to change out of their street clothes and into their costumes in the ladies' bathroom. Except that the bathroom is usually crowded, too. Sometimes, it feels like every girl in the competition is in there, fighting for space in front of the mirror to do her hair and her makeup. Everyone is always bumping someone else with an elbow or a curling iron, and the air is so thick with clouds of hairspray and mousse, you can hardly see your fingers in front of your face.

The stands are filled not with fans, but with nervous parents and jittery skaters dressed in sweat suits and warm-up jackets waiting for their event to start. The only cameras belong to Mom and Dad, and one video-camera operator hired to record the entire event. If you want to watch how you skated afterward, you don't wait for your program to be shown on TV. You buy a copy of it from the camera operator.

There's no electronic scoreboard flashing the marks. Results are posted on a printed piece of paper on a wall next to the bathrooms. As soon as one event is over, the anxious competitors, their coaches, and their parents gather around it, jabbering nervously, chewing on their nails, jumping from foot to foot, and waiting for an official to emerge from the office and tape up the rankings for everyone to read. Someone is always grinning with surprise and hugging everyone around them, and someone is always crying.

But just because a regional competition isn't as glamorous or as well attended as a World or National Championship doesn't mean the skaters who participate in it are any less excited, any less worried, or any less dedicated to their sport.

When Sarah competed at the 1996 North Atlantics, she was as determined to skate her best as she would be years later, standing by the barrier in Canada, waiting for her turn to step on the ice. She knew that a good skate there would lead to competing at the Eastern Sectionals, and then, possibly, the Nationals, to be held that year in San Jose, California.

And, even though she was only ten years old, Sarah skated well enough to finish third in the North Atlantic region. She did qualify for the Eastern Sectional.

There, however, she unfortunately only placed tenth. Six long places away from going to Nationals.

Among the girls from Easterns who did qualify to go that year was Erin Pearl, from Maine. Sarah didn't know it yet, but she'd be seeing Erin again.

However, with Easterns over, Sarah had a choice to make. She could take the test that would qualify her to skate with the Junior ladies and move up a level, or she could stay a Novice and try to make the Nationals again in 1997.

Robin was honest with Sarah. She let her know how good she was, but she also let her know that Sarah was capable of a lot more.

As a result, Sarah decided to stay a Novice, figuring she would have a whole other year to work on her jumps and her spins and her presentation to try to make the Nationals in Nashville, Tennessee.

And Sarah was right—in a way. She did improve during that second year at Novice. She improved enough to, this time, win the North Atlantic Regionals and get her picture in *Skating Magazine*, holding the gold medal and smiling.

Sarah was thrilled. Her goal, after all, is always to move up each year, to keep improving and moving up the ranks.

But, when she got to the Easterns, all of her moving up still wasn't enough. Sarah finished in sixth place. Good enough to be named second alternate to Nationals. Good enough to have to stay, tired and yawning, after the event and fill out all of her paperwork just in case someone else couldn't make it, and Sarah got to compete after all. But, sixth place wasn't good enough to go to Nashville.

Still, in spite of the not-good-enough result, Sarah, to this day, insists that she learns from every competition, from what she did well and from those things that she realizes she could do better. The results aren't something she dwells on.

Unfortunately, that time the results dictated that, for the second year in a row, Sarah stayed home and watched the Nationals on TV.

The girl who won the 1997 U.S. National Novice title was a tiny Korean-American spitfire named Naomi Nari Nam. Sarah would be seeing a lot more of her in future years, as well.

But, now, it was time for Sarah to make another choice. Stay Novice for a third year, or move up to Juniors? It was a tough call. Going by how much Sarah had improved from 1996 to 1997, it wasn't unreasonable to assume that, if she stayed Novice, she just might make it to Nationals the next year. And, once she was there, Sarah would be one of the more experienced Novice girls. After skating in Novice for three years, Sarah had a chance to win the whole thing.

Robin and Sarah carefully weighed their options. Together with her parents, Robin tried to offer her top pupil balance. From the start, they'd all been careful not to set goals that were too big. Because they all knew how very easy it was to get caught up in near-term opportunities.

Sometimes it could be a little too much. That's where everyone drew the line. From Sarah's first day on the ice to her most recent World Championship, everybody's first consideration is always, "What will let Sarah have the best opportunity to reach her maximum potential?" There are no second or third considerations.

If Sarah moved up to Juniors, she'd be the underdog again. Not only would she be one of the youngest and one of the newest girls on the scene, but she'd also be competing against skaters like Erin Pearl and Naomi Nari Nam, girls who'd already been to Nationals and won medals there. What kind of chance would Sarah have as a Junior?

And yet, doing another year of Novice, well, that seemed kind of . . . boring.

So after a lot of thinking and weighing and talking, the decision was made: even though she'd never made it to Nationals as a Novice, Sarah Hughes would be throwing caution to the wind and, for the 1997–1998 season, skating as a Junior.

They'd try their best, and they'd see what happened. It would be a very busy and hard year.

Unfortunately, nobody could have predicted just how hard.

Moving up a whole level was supposed to be the most difficult thing twelve-year-old Sarah would have to deal with that year.

But that was before Sarah's mother came to her with some truly frightening news.

CHAPTER FOUR

Ladies' Skating: The Jumping Beans

SARAH Hughes's first memory of watching skating on television was Kristi Yamaguchi winning the Olympic gold medal in Albertville, France, in 1992. Born and raised in northern California, Kristi was the quintessential example of the new breed of skater. Triple jumps were the name of the game, and Kristi could jump with the best of them.

At the 1990 World Championships, the last year that compulsory figures—circular patterns traced and retraced into the ice with precision—were part of the score, Kristi could finish no higher than fourth place. A year later, in 1991, with no compulsory figures to slow her down, Kristi Yamaguchi triple-jumped her way to a world championship.

Like Sarah, Kristi came from a close-knit athletic family. Brother Brett played basketball. Sister Lori was a world champion baton twirler. And, like Sarah, Kristi stuck with one coach, Christy Ness, for most of her career. She even lived at home with her family for the bulk of her skating years, only moving up north to Canada with Christy toward the very end, to finish her training for the Olympics.

After becoming the first American woman since Dorothy Hamill in 1976 to win the Olympics, Kristi joined Scott Hamilton's skating tour, "Stars on Ice," and traveled the world, performing in shows and professional competitions.

The bronze medalist at the 1992 Olympics, Nancy Kerrigan, also had much in common with Sarah. Nancy too followed her hockey-playing brothers onto the ice, then made the switch to figure skating.

Although a solid jumper, Nancy wasn't the most consistent competitor, and she became better known for her elegant, sophisticated look on the ice. When skating fans talked about her strengths, it was usually Nancy's grace and long, classic lines that came up in conversation, not her jumps.

The year before the 1992 Olympics, Nancy was a surprise bronze medalist at the 1991 World Championships. She found herself on the podium after medal favorite and 1989 World Champion Midori Ito suffered a freak fall straight through the boards surrounding the rink. However, after her bronze at the Olympics, skating pundits began to think that maybe Nancy wasn't a fluke after all. Even if she didn't have the big jumps like Midori Ito or 1991 U.S. Champion Tonya Harding, maybe she still could challenge for the World Championship.

But, at the 1993 World Championships, Nancy completely fell apart. She won the Short Program but skated so badly in the Long that she tumbled down to fifth place.

"I just want to die," Nancy sobbed to her coach on live television.

Heading into the 1994 Olympics, a medal seemed unlikely for Nancy. She was only a favorite for the 1994 U.S. title because her primary competition, Tonya Harding, was also skating badly that year (and no one really expected much from that adorable, tiny Michelle Kwan).

But then, at the 1994 U.S. Nationals, a man later revealed to be working for Tonya Harding's husband viciously clubbed Nancy on the knee. Her story was carried on news programs all over the planet, and soon, everyone in the world was wondering if Nancy Kerrigan would be able to recover in time for the Olympics.

Overnight, she went from being a name only hard-core skating fans knew to the girl everyone wanted to see. Ironically, she became a star in those few weeks between Nationals and Olympics when she wasn't skating at all.

The day Nancy Kerrigan stepped on Olympic ice, the whole world seemed to be watching. The television ratings for women's figure skating were the highest they'd ever been.

And, in spite of the tension, in spire of the scrutiny, the young woman who only a year earlier had been so nervous to be sitting in the favorite position for a medal that she completely fell apart, gave the performance of her life. It was almost as if getting hit on the knee somehow finally gave Nancy the drive and the guts she'd always needed to perform under pressure. She skated marvelously at the Olympics, winning the Short Program and only making one mistake in the Long, to finish second overall in one of the most hotly debated and closest contests ever.

Afterward, Nancy also joined the professional skating world, skating in her own shows and others' professional competitions, as well as getting married and becoming the proud mother of a son, Matthew.

Meanwhile, the woman who beat Nancy for the gold in Lillehammer, Ukraine's Oksana Baiul, wasn't living quite as happily-of-an-ever-after.

After her mother and grandmother died when she was a little girl, Oksana moved in with her coach, Galina Zmievskaya, while she trained for the Olympics. However, after winning the gold, the success and fame seemed to go to Oksana's head. Without a strong family to support her the way most past champions had been loved and supported, Oksana found herself drinking too much, even though she wasn't old enough yet to be legally drinking at all. Eventually, she was involved in a drunk driving accident, injuring both herself and the friend in the car with her.

Some thought being arrested by the police might finally get Oksana the help she needed. But, help can only be given to someone who wants to take it. Even though Oksana gave lip service to wanting to pull her life together, she couldn't quite seem to settle down. After firing the coach who'd been like a mother to her growing up, Oksana flitted about from one trainer to another to the detriment

of her career. Though she still periodically talks of rein-
stating and trying for another Olympic gold, the odds
seemed very much against her.

If for no other reason than the fact that, even if she
could still land the jumps she completed to win the 1994
Olympics, Oksana would be out of her technical league. In
her absence from the eligible scene, the ladies' technical
level catapulted another huge notch at the 1998 Olympics
when defending World Champion Tara Lipinski landed
two triple-triple combinations in her long program in Na-
gano.

Like Kristi Yamaguchi and Midori Ito, Tara was another
of the new breed of skaters. She was another jumping prod-
igy.

One month after her twelfth birthday, Tara won the
1994 U.S. Olympic festival, becoming the youngest Festival
medalist ever.

Half a year later, in 1995, she finished second at the
U.S. Junior National Championship, and fourth at the Junior Worlds.

In 1996, she dropped down to fifth place at the Junior
Worlds, but in an upset over the 1995 World Junior Champion Sydne Vogel, placed third at the National Championships, qualifying herself for a spot on the 1996 World
Championship team.

There, apparently overwhelmed to be competing at her
first World Championship, Tara made mistake after mistake in her short program, finishing in twenty-third place,
one spot away from not even qualifying to skate the Long

Program. But, after a day to pull herself together, Tara came back with a vengeance. She skated her personal best in the Long Program, giving the judges no choice but to rank her eleventh, ahead of people like the Hungarian National Champion, the French National Champion, the Swiss National Champion, the Canadian National Champion, and the Ukrainian National Champion. Between her twenty-third place in the Short Program and her eleventh place in the Long, Tara finished fifteenth overall.

Then, a year later, Tara Lipinski won the whole thing. At only fifteen years old, she actually won the 1997 World Championship!

From fifteenth place to first in one year. It was one of the biggest jumps up the standings in figure skating history.

Unlike Sarah Hughes and so many of the women who came before her, Tara, it seems, won her gold medals with seemingly no waiting at all.

CHAPTER FIVE

Off-Ice Heartbreak

SARAH Hughes waited.

Earlier, her mother had said she had something important to tell all six of her children: Rebecca, David, Matt, Sarah, and the littlest ones, Emily and Taylor. She told them she was going to be totally honest. Because Amy Hughes didn't believe in secrets. She preferred letting her kids know exactly what was going on.

And what was going on was that Sarah's mother had breast cancer.

Breast cancer is one of the most awful diseases that can strike a woman. It usually starts as a lump a woman can feel in her breast. The lump can be hot or it can be hard or it can be painful. Sometimes, it can feel like nothing at all, but it should always be taken seriously. There are different kinds of lumps. Some lumps are benign, which means they're harmless. They can be taken out with surgery and then everything is okay again. But, some lumps are malignant. Which means they're growing. And a growing lump is very, very dangerous.

A growing lump means the disease is definitely cancer. And cancer means cells growing out of control. These malignant, growing cells can get into the blood, then spread to other areas of the body and start growing there. The spread of cancer is called metastasis. And, once it starts, it gets harder and harder to catch and stop. Some of the most dangerous places for cancer to spread and grow is in the lungs, making it impossible to breathe, or in the brain, making it impossible to function or move at all. That's why the worst thing that can happen with cancer is for it to be allowed to spread. Because there are places where cancer, once it has settled in, can't be taken out, not even with surgery. To get better, cancer absolutely has to be stopped before it spreads.

Sarah listened very carefully to what her mother was saying. She heard the words cancer and surgery. And then she heard another word: chemotherapy.

Chemotherapy is the injection of specific drugs into the blood stream in an attempt to kill the cancer cells and keep them from spreading. Unfortunately, the drugs can't tell the difference between sick cells and healthy ones, and, as a result, affect normal cells as well. This is one of the worst side effects of cancer treatment. Because anticancer drugs affect rapidly dividing cells, it means they affect the blood cells which fight infection, help the blood to clot, and carry oxygen to all parts of the body. When blood cells are affected, women receiving chemotherapy are more likely to get infections, may bruise or bleed easily, and may feel unusually weak and very tired. Cells in their hair roots and cells that line the digestive tract may also be affected. As a result, other awful side effects include loss of hair, poor appetite, nausea, vomiting, diarrhea, or mouth and lip sores. Chemotherapy can be very effective at treating cancer, but it is also a very, very difficult and painful way to do it.

Knowing all that, knowing that all of that might soon happen to her, Sarah's mother tried to explain chemotherapy the best that she could to all of her kids.

But, even though it was pretty horrible, for Sarah, hearing the word was actually a relief.

Oh, chemotherapy, Sarah thought, Mom would be all right then. Scott Hamilton went through the same thing.

Sarah was thinking about the 1984 Olympic and four-time World Champion, Scott Hamilton, who in 1997 told the world that, like Sarah's mother, he had cancer, too.

In Scott's case, the disease was testicular cancer, a cancer that struck only men just like breast cancer mostly happened to women. But still, the treatment for it was the same. Scott Hamilton underwent extensive chemotherapy. The drugs made his hair fall out. They made him so sick and weak that he could barely walk, much less skate.

In the end, though, Scott Hamilton did recover. In fact, he got so well that, in October of 1997, he starred in a television special called *Scott Hamilton: Back on the Ice.* After he finished skating his comeback number, the still bald, but fully recovered Scott looked at the audience who'd come to welcome him back to skating, raised one fist in the air and triumphantly shouted, "I win!"

Sarah knew that if Scott Hamilton could beat cancer, well then certainly her mom, who was just as strong and brave and determined as the champion ice skater, could do it, too. Sarah told her mom she had nothing to worry about. Sarah was sure she'd be okay.

"I wanted to call up Scott Hamilton and just kiss him," Amy Hughes laughed to www.USFSA.org. "Someone my daughter knew of and admired so much had been through cancer and beat it."

Now, it would be Amy's turn to do the same thing.

No matter how worried she was about her mother's illness, Sarah decided she would keep training, keep skating, and hopefully make her mother proud.

Sarah had always considered herself a pretty motivated person before, but now, she and Robin decided they would be even more motivated. Since this would be Sarah's first year on the Junior level, she would work even harder than she had as a Novice, working to refine her jumps, as well as all of the moves she and Robin call the "in-betweens."

To that end, Sarah and Robin devoted more practice time to refining Sarah's artistry and presentation. It was vitally important to them that people see how she'd improved her presentation level and musicality. Robin was sure that Sarah's athletic ability, combined with her very balletic appearance on the ice, would work well together and make her very pleasant to watch.

Now, all they needed was for the judges to agree.

And, in the fall of 1997, they finally did!

After not even making it to Nationals in Novice, Sarah won both the 1998 North Atlantic Junior Regionals, and the 1998 Eastern Junior Sectionals. At twelve years old, she was on her way to Philadelphia for the 1998 United States Nationals!

NATIONALS, of course, is always a very exciting competition. But, once every four years, it becomes even more exciting. That's because, once every four years, the skaters aren't just competing for medals and a chance to go to Worlds, they're competing for a chance to represent the United States at the Winter Olympic Games.

As a Junior skater, Sarah knew she had no chance of making the 1998 Olympic team. Those spots were only open for Senior skaters. Still, it was exciting just to be there and watch.

What made Sarah sad, though, was that her mother wasn't there to do the same thing. Amy Hughes was in the hospital, receiving the chemotherapy she'd told her kids about months ago. She was too sick and weak to travel with Sarah and be at Nationals with her all week like most of the other kids' moms had.

So, Sarah's dad came, as well as her siblings. They sat

in the arena while she practiced, and cheered her on during her short program, which, to a lot of experts' surprise, Sarah won.

And then, something miraculous happened. Even though she was in the middle of a long and debilitating treatment, Amy Hughes crawled out of her hospital bed, and, using all of her strength, made the effort to come to Philadelphia just for one night to watch Sarah skate the Junior Ladies' Long Program.

Amy later said that for the few minutes she was sitting in the arena, watching her daughter on the ice performing the routine she'd been working on for so long, Amy Hughes felt perfectly well.

And she felt even better when Sarah won the Long Program and was crowned the 1998 U.S. Junior Ladies' Champion! (Beating, among others, the previous year's Novice Champion, Naomi Nari Nam.)

As *International Figure Skating* wrote in its February 1999 issue, "Sarah Hughes' first place finish at the 1998 U.S. Nationals in the junior women's competition confirmed what her friends and family have known for a long time— that her hard work and love for skating could translate into medals."

AFTER Sarah's win at Nationals, her life and her skating suddenly kicked up a notch. A year earlier, no one even knew who she was. Now, the United States Figure Skating Association (USFSA) was inviting Sarah to travel overseas and compete against some of the best Junior-level skaters from other countries. The USFSA wanted Sarah to become part of the Junior Grand Prix circuit, a series of competitions all over the world. Skaters went from country to country, taking part in different meets and collecting points based on how well they did at each one. The six skaters who got the most points over the course of a season then qualified to compete at the Junior Grand Prix Final.

Even though she was barely thirteen years old, Sarah was ready for the challenge.

Her first stop was Budapest, Hungary, and the Hungarian Trophy competition. She finished second and won the silver medal.

While in Hungary, in her spare time, Sarah did some sightseeing, some shopping, and, so as not to get bored, she brought her schoolwork along, too.

Considering how much of her life revolves around skating, Sarah admits that sometimes it's hard to think about anything else. But, the last thing Sarah wants is to fall into the trap of starting to believe that absolutely everything and everyone revolves around ice and landing triple jumps. That's why she's so dedicated to her schoolwork. As long as she's writing a paper or working on a math problem, she can focus on something outside of the sport. Schoolwork, she explains, helps her put the world into perspective.

After Hungary, next on Sarah's competition schedule was the Mexico Cup in Mexico City, Mexico. Once again, she finished second. As an added bonus, traveling to Mex-

ico gave Sarah the chance to try out on the locals the Spanish she'd been studying for three years. At least, that was
the plan. It didn't quite turn out that way. Sarah discovered
that as badly as she wanted to practice her Spanish on the
Mexicans, the Mexicans wanted to practice their English
on her!

Then, in December, after she won their selection competition in Chicago, the USFSA sent Sarah to Zagreb, Croatia, to compete at the World Junior Figure Skating
Championship.

It was the most important competition of the year for
Junior-level skaters. And a good indicator of which girls
might have the stuff to go even further in their sport.

After all, five women who'd won the Junior World
Championship then went on to win the Senior World
Championship. There was America's Elaine Zayak (Junior
Worlds in 1979 and Senior Worlds in 1982), America's Ros-
alynn Sumners (1980/1983), America's Kristi Yamaguchi
(1988/1991 and 1992), Japan's Yuka Sato (1990/1994) and
America's Michelle Kwan, who won the Junior World
Championship in 1994, and her first Senior title two years
later. Overall, nine American women had won the Junior
World title, more than from any other country.

In 1998, forty-four girls from thirty-nine different countries were entered in the prestigious event. The favorite to
win was Russia's Viktoria Volchkova. She'd surprised everyone at the 1998 Goodwill Games by winning the bronze
medal among the Senior Ladies, and she had already competed at the World Junior Championships a year earlier,
winning the bronze medal there, as well.

Yet, much to many people's surprise, Sarah Hughes managed to not only win her qualifying round and beat Viktoria there, but she also ended up beating Viktoria overall. On her very first try, Sarah Hughes finished second at the Junior World Championship. Russia's Daria Timoshenko won the event. Viktoria Volchkova finished third.

Robin was ecstatic.

"When she won U.S. Juniors last year," Robin told *The Augusta Chronicle*, "I thought, 'OK, she's taken that first, small step.' Then, when she was second at Junior Worlds, I said, 'Now she's taken that second step.' Juniors is really just the beginning. Her winning Juniors put her into the arena where she can really further her career."

But, for Sarah, the best part of the event wasn't the silver medal or the knowledge that her performance would be shown on television in the United States on ESPN. The best part was that, finally, her mom was well enough to travel again.

She and the rest of the Hughes brood flew overseas to support Sarah, and the family shared a traditional American Thanksgiving—in Zagreb, Croatia.

Her silver medals in Budapest and Mexico City earned Sarah enough points to qualify for the Junior Grand Prix Final, to be held in Detroit, Michigan, in March of 1999. But, first, it was once again time for Sarah to make an important decision.

Should she stay a Junior skater for another year, or should she take the plunge and move up to the Senior level? Internationally, she could only compete as a Junior because of her age, but in the U.S. the difference between Junior and Senior wasn't age, but still level. As long as she passed the Senior test, she could skate as a Senior lady in the U.S., including at the National Championships.

Again, there were good reasons for doing both.

If Sarah moved up to Seniors, she would be among the youngest girls in her group. She would need to add an extra thirty seconds to her long program. (Junior Ladies skate a program three and a half minutes in length, while Senior Ladies' programs are four minutes long.) It may not have sounded like much, but that extra thirty seconds meant more jumps, more spins, plain old more skating, and a heck of a lot more endurance.

If Sarah stayed Junior she could keep the long program, "Swan Lake," that she'd been working on all year, the one she used to win all those silver medals in Budapest, Mexico City, and Zagreb. She could also return to the Junior World Championships the following year and take another crack at the gold medal.

It was a tough choice to make, and, once again, the decision fell to Sarah and Robin.

For her part, Robin was very careful not to expect too much of Sarah too soon. She believed that such a nice-and-easy attitude was the key to keeping Sarah from expecting too much too soon of herself. And she was right. Robin's realistic and practical approach to all things skating usually helped make Sarah's decisions easier. To Robin, that meant that Team Hughes was on the right track.

Sarah thought they were on the right track, too. That's

why she, realistically and practically, made her decision: She would move up to Seniors.

Sarah's reasons were simple. She didn't want to go back to Juniors because there was nowhere for her to go in Juniors but down. All she could do in Juniors was either win again—serious been there, done that, action—or she could lose. Losing wasn't any fun. Besides, the more Senior competition experience, the better.

And so it was all set. Sarah would compete as a Senior Lady at the 1999 U.S. Nationals. She would add the thirty seconds to her program, and she would go for it.

But, at the same time, Sarah's silver medals in Hungary and Mexico had won her enough points to qualify for the Junior Grand Prix Final to be held after the Nationals. And the Junior Grand Prix Final required a Junior-level long program.

Not a problem—Sarah would train both! She would practice both "Swan Lake" the three-and-a-half minute version, and "Swan Lake" the four-minute cut.

"And those 30 seconds (felt) like a lot!" she kidded to *International Figure Skating.*

It would mean double the work (not to mention always being afraid that, in the middle of a performance, she would forget which program it was she was supposed to be doing). But, Sarah was up to giving it a whirl. So, unlike a majority of the girls she'd be skating against, Sarah diligently practiced not one long program, but two every day.

"We'll just take one competition at a time," Robin added, "Whether it's a junior or a senior event, and concentrate on it."

There was also the matter of maturity. The kind of artistry and presentation that Sarah won medals with on the Junior level might very well not be enough when she was slugging it out with the Senior Ladies.

On the Senior level, Sarah would be skating against people like 1998 Olympic Silver Medalist Michelle Kwan, who is world-famous for her grace, beauty, and poise.

She'd be up against Angela Nikodinov, an Olympic alternate known for her "theme" programs; programs that told an entire story from beginning to end, like the one where she reenacted the fairy tale of Cinderella with her skating, while also landing difficult double and triple jumps.

Sarah wondered if her version of *Swan Lake* would be able to measure up. What if the judges looked out on the ice, and sniffed that they just saw a little girl bouncing around with no sense of grace, style, or grown-up passion?

Robin tried to reassure her top student, reminding Sarah to be herself. As she explained to *The Augusta Chronicle*:

"There's only so much passion you can expect out of a thirteen-year-old. She is so young that I didn't want to do anything that was extremely passionate or deep in emotion, and yet, her two pieces of music ("Fantasy Impromptu" by Frederic Chopin for the Short Program and "Swan Lake" for the Long) are that, as a young skater, she could interpret and feel comfortable skating to, and still grow with throughout the year."

And Sarah agreed. Up to a point.

"It's a fine line," she admitted. "You try to be yourself, but you don't want to skate like a child, either. I don't want to act fifteen or twenty."

Which meant that it was time for Sarah Hughes to find out if acting thirteen would be good enough.

THE 1999 U.S. Figure Skating Nationals were held in Salt Lake City, at the same rink where the Olympics were scheduled to take place in 2002. The venue was pretty inspirational for Sarah.

Like every other skater, Sarah had always dreamed of going to the Olympics. She had thought it might, just might be possible in 2002, but, to be honest, she didn't think she'd be where she was at that moment, in 1999.

And these particular Nationals were shaping up to be a pretty exciting competition. Even before anyone had stepped out onto the ice, the press was taking guesses over who the top ladies might be at the end of the week. Everyone agreed that, barring a disaster, Michelle Kwan would win the gold yet again. But, what about the rest of the podium? 1998 Olympic Champion Tara Lipinski had retired. 1995 U.S. Champion and World Bronze Medalist Nicole Bobek was out sick. So who did that leave to battle for the medals?

Could it be Angela Nikodinov, who almost made it to Worlds the previous year? How about Amber Corwin, who in 1997 became the first and only American woman to land a triple-triple combination in her short program? How about Naomi Nari Nam? Or Erin Pearl?

Or how about, an Associated Press article asked, that young Sarah Hughes? "She has athletic ability and a budding gracefulness, not to mention a couple of impressive titles. She just might have what it takes."

Sarah took all the compliments and predictions in stride.

She knew she couldn't go out with horribly high expectations because then the pressure she put on herself would surely do her in. So Sarah decided that she would just go out and treat it like any other competition. After all, it would be lame to go out screaming, "Oh, my gosh, it's the world juniors!" Or, "Oh, my gosh, it's Senior Nationals!" She would just do what she could do because that was the only thing she had any control over.

As always, Sarah's family was in Salt Lake City to cheer her on. Looking back to the previous year, her mother was even able to find the silver lining in her illness.

"Sarah understands everything better now," Amy told *The Daily News.* "My problems put things in perspective."

The truth was, after watching her mother go through surgery and chemotherapy and seeing her feeling so sick and weak afterward that she could barely get out of bed, Sarah just wasn't that intimidated taking the ice at Nationals. Not even in practice, where the newly Senior thirteen-year-old was surrounded on all sides by more experienced girls, by girls she'd previously only seen on television or from a distance.

It was also her first time skating in a big arena. Robin

could tell that Sarah was still feeling herself out in the new surroundings and that she needed to skate a good practice session to feel totally comfortable.

"Just remember," Robin told her, hoping to psyche Sarah up and make her feel more at home, "You belong here like everyone else."

Even when that "everyone else" included Michelle Kwan.

"I just didn't want to (crash) into her," Sarah giggled at a later press conference. "I think every girl who goes to Seniors for the first time walks in the dressing room and thinks, 'Oh my God! There's Michelle Kwan!' My problem was that I almost blurted out, 'Oh my God! There's Michelle Kwan!' "

Still, when a friendly Michelle Kwan skated up to Sarah to make polite conversation and ask Sarah if she was missing her school's finals by coming to Nationals, Sarah held her composure, even though her stomach was doing flip-flops, and explained that no, she wasn't.

Surprised, Michelle asked, "What grade are you in?"

"Eighth."

"Oh, my gosh!" Michelle exclaimed in recognition.

Michelle and Sarah certainly had a lot in common. When Michelle was thirteen, she was already skating at her second U.S. Nationals as a Senior lady. But, just like with Sarah, all anyone could talk about was "aw, look at that cute, bouncy little girl trying to hold her own against the Senior Ladies."

That year, 1994, the cute, bouncy little girl won the silver medal and was named alternate to the Olympic Team.

That's why, five years later, Michelle Kwan, better than anyone, knew never to underestimate a cute, bouncy little eighth-grader.

CHAPTER SIX

The Competition: Russia

FOR most skaters just getting to compete at Nationals is the biggest goal of the year. They dream about it, they work for it, and, once it's over, they take a long-deserved vacation.

But, for an elite few, Nationals is just the beginning. For them, Nationals is only one part of the battle to be waged on the way to skating fame and fortune.

Sure, proving you're the best in America and securing a place on the U.S. World Team, is terrific. It's an amazing achievement. One that only a tiny percentage of all the skaters in the United States will ever experience. But, unlike the majority who, after Nationals, take off for Hawaii or Disney World or just home for a good night's sleep, the skaters who've qualified for the world team get to enjoy their medals for about twenty-four hours. And then it's back to the rink. Because, in about six weeks or so, it will be time to tackle that next step on the ladder of skating achievement: taking on the world.

The International Skating Union (ISU) boasts over fifty member countries, and all of them are eligible to send at least one skater to the World Championship. Skaters from countries as far away as New Zealand, Israel, Australia, Croatia, South Africa, and China regularly come to test their abilities against the best in the world.

But, in twenty-first-century women's skating, taking on the world in the hopes of winning a medal means taking on the Russians.

This wasn't always the case.

In the beginning, Hungary was the country to beat in Ladies' Skating. From 1908 to 1914, two different Hungarian girls won all the World Championship gold medals. Then it was Austria's turn. Then Norway, courtesy of Sonja Henie, of course.

After Sonja retired in 1936, the World title bounced between Great Britain, Canada, the United States, France, and Holland, with Germany sneaking onto the scene in 1969. While Russians won a majority of the gold, silver, and bronze medals in pairs and ice dance, and even fielded a men's world champion in 1975, 1977 and 1985, no Russian girl even won a medal at the World Championship until Elena Vodorezova earned the bronze in 1983.

Skating experts felt it was because the pairs and dance programs in Russia were considered to be the more prestigious ones. Pair skaters like two-time Olympic Gold Medalist Ludmilla Belousova and three-time Olympic Gold Medalist Irina Rodnina were the skating stars Russians flocked to. So, naturally, the best girls were directed into the pairs and ice-dancing programs, leaving the less talented ones to flounder in a weak Singles program. It made sense, in a way. The Soviet Union was a Communist country. They valued teamwork above individuality. Naturally then, they'd want to promote pairs and dance, disciplines that proved the benefits of working together, versus Single skating, which is all about the individual.

Nevertheless, Elena Vodorezova was followed by Anna Kondrashova (Silver) at the 1984 Worlds and Kira Ivanova (Silver) in 1985.

But, it wasn't until Irina Slutskaya became the first Russian woman to win the European Championship in 1996 then followed that victory up with a bronze medal at that year's World Championship, that Russia actually had a bonafide, long-term contender on the scene.

For Irina Slutskaya, ice-skating was something her mother forced her into because the sickly four-year-old was prone to colds and coughs, and doctors thought the fresh, cold air would do her good. From the beginning, Irina's parents were one hundred percent supportive of her career, even giving up their two-bedroom Moscow apartment to move into a much smaller one that was closer to the rink.

Like Sarah, Irina has worked with one key coach for her entire career. Coach Zhanna Gromova remembers a little girl back in group-lessons, all bundled up in layers and layers of warm clothes, rosy-cheeked and full of energy. In fact, little Irina had so much energy, her grandmother used to call her a typhoon!

Together, Zhanna and Irina's first major victory was the bronze medal at the 1994 World Junior Championship, behind America's Michelle Kwan. Then, in 1995, Irina herself won the title. She made a huge splash at "Skate America" that year, winning the Short Program ahead of European and French Champion Surya Bonaly. But, the pressure of being the leader got to her, and Irina skated an error-filled program to drop down to third place.

"She got too nervous," her mother said later. "That's her problem. She wanted it too much."

And then, her mother revealed that the one thing Irina wanted more than anything following the 1994 World Juniors, was to beat the girl she saw as the ultimate skater, Michelle Kwan.

Irina set beating Michelle as her goal, and she approached it in 1996, when she won the bronze medal in Edmonton, Canada, the same year that Michelle won her first World Championship.

Then, in 1997, Irina, despite landing a triple-triple combination at the World Championship, could only finish fourth to Michelle's second (Irina had suffered a fall in the Short Program after injuring her back in practice, and just couldn't catch up to Michelle in the Long Program). At the Olympics in 1998, an unhappy and unmotivated Irina dropped one more spot, to fifth, while Michelle was again second.

The shock of doing poorly at the Olympics seemed to shake Irina up a little, and she made a bit of a comeback at the 1998 World Championships a month later, finishing second to Michelle's first. But, after that, Irina's career truly seemed to go downhill.

She gained weight. She got depressed. She skated badly. In 1999, the European champion and two-time World medalist could only finish fourth at her own Russian Nationals. (Despite her World medals, Irina had never up to that point managed to win a National title. Her mother thought it was because Irina skated too much like a young, energetic girl, and Russian Nationals judges preferred a more smooth, balletic, mature style.) In 1999, after a disastrous Nationals, Irina didn't even qualify for the World Championship team and had to stay home, watching it on TV.

She considered quitting. Skating was becoming too hard, and too heartbreaking. For most girls, skating was their joy, but, for Irina, it had become a job. And a job she didn't even really like.

But, then again, quitting wasn't something Irina really liked, either. Besides, after everything her family had sacrificed, she felt she owed it to them to keep trying. Not to mention that the money she made skating in one competition was more than her parents could ever hope to earn in a year. Irina was the one supporting them, now. She couldn't quit. She just couldn't.

And so, instead of quitting, Irina took up jogging, hoping to get back into competitive shape. While jogging, she met a young man, seven years older than her, named Sergei Mikheeyev.

They wed in August of 1999.

And suddenly everything changed for Irina.

Newly married, newly fit, newly happy, skating finally turned back into the pleasure it had once been. She blew back onto the competitive circuit with a vengeance. During the 1999–2000 season, Irina won one of her Grand Prix events and placed third at the other. And then she won the Grand Prix Final.

Ahead of Michelle Kwan.

It took her five years, but, finally, Irina had achieved her goal.

Which, naturally meant that it was time for a new one. Now that she'd beaten Michelle in competition, Irina had her eyes set on the ultimate prize: A World Championship title.

She was the favorite heading into the 2000 Worlds.

But, it wasn't to be.

Irina did not skate her best in Nice, France. Michelle Kwan did. Michelle won the gold, Irina the silver.

Disappointed, Irina vowed that 2001 would be her year.

And it almost was.

Irina again won all three of her Grand Prix events in the 2000–2001 season, this time even beating Michelle Kwan at two separate competitions. She again won the Grand Prix Final over Michelle. Naturally, she was an even heavier favorite to win it all in Canada at the Worlds. But, again, it wasn't to be.

Irina, like her mother observed all those years ago, "wanted it too much." She made mistakes, while Michelle skated brilliantly. Michelle won the gold. Irina won the silver.

Their next major meeting will be in Salt Lake City, at the 2002 Olympic Games. Where both young women will be at their hungriest.

✳

✳ NOT that Irina and Michelle will be the only ladies in Salt Lake City contesting for the gold. Irina's teammate and main Russian competitor, Maria Butyrskaya, fully intends to throw her hat into the rink at what will definitely be her last Olympics, and maybe her very last eligible event ever. If Maria is coming to Salt Lake City with a bit more confidence than most of the other competitors, it is probably because, unlike any other girl planning to be there, Maria has already beaten both Michelle and Irina in competition.

It's very possible that Maria might be the oldest woman skating in Salt Lake City. She will arguably be the one with the most experience.

Like Irina, Maria also started ice-skating at the urging of her mother, who wanted to keep her active five-year-old occupied, and there just happened to be an ice rink near her house.

Unlike Irina and Sarah, however, Maria went through numerous coaches in her career, and success did not come at an early age.

Still, she was determined to succeed.

As a tiny ten-year-old, she was urged to take up Pair skating. But, Maria had loftier goals. Whenever anyone tried to talk her into being a Pair skater, she would insist, "No. I'm going to be the first Russian World Champion in Ladies' Singles."

Easier said than done.

At her first World Championship, in 1993, Maria did not make it out of her qualifying group. Because she was the only Russian woman there, Russia lost their chance to send a woman to the 1994 Olympics. And, after that happened, Maria felt like the Russia Skating Federation decided she was all washed up, and put all their eggs in "the Irina Slutskaya basket."

Nevertheless, Maria won the Russian National Championship for the third time in 1996 (beating Irina) and headed off to Worlds in Edmonton. She finished fourth. A most respectable result.

Except that, in 1996, Irina finished third.

The triple jumps just seemed to come so easily to Irina.

"Of course." Maria shrugged. "Everything is easy at fifteen. Just wait until she tries to do it with a grown woman's body."

Because, unlike practically everyone else she was skating against, Maria was a grown woman. She was twenty-five at the 1998 Olympics.

She finished fourth, just out of the medals. (She did, however, beat Irina to prove that, in Russia at least, youth wasn't everything.)

And she was twenty-six in 1999.

When she became the oldest woman to ever win the World Championship.

It was not only a dream come true for Maria, but a personal validation, as well. She'd been in the lead after the Short Program, and, with Michelle Kwan sitting in fourth, Maria only had to be second in the Long Program to win the whole thing. Her coach, wanting Maria to skate clean and make no mistakes, urged her not to do her final triple loop. While Maria skated, her coach yelled from the boards for her to skip the final jump, she didn't need it! But, Maria was determined to win not by default, but by skating the competition of her life.

And that was exactly what she did.

Unfortunately, winning Worlds proved to be a bit of a curse for Maria. The following year, she was so worried about skating up to what she thought were standards judges expected from a World Champion, that she was nervous and unsure and constantly looking over her shoulder, wondering what people were thinking about her and whether they were whispering that she'd won her title unfairly.

The constant worrying weighed heavily on Maria's shoulders, and, at the 2000 World Championships, she only skated well enough to place third, after Michelle Kwan and Irina Slutskaya.

Then, in 2001, Maria Butyrskaya, the oldest woman in the event and the reigning World Bronze Medalist failed to defend her title. She finished in fourth place and out of the medals.

It wasn't a very good omen for the Olympics. But, Maria Butyrskaya has come back from defeat before. If, like she promises, the 2002 Olympics are scheduled to be her last competition, odds are she's going to give it everything she's got.

In Salt Lake City, Sarah Hughes won't only be competing against the defending World Champion, Michelle Kwan, she'll be skating against two Russian women who both have a lot to prove.

CHAPTER SEVEN

World Class

SARAH Hughes waited.

This was it. This was the big time. The 1999 U.S. National Championships, Senior Ladies' Short Program.

Her whole family was in the stands, watching, just like they always were when Sarah competed. To Sarah, it was kind of funny to know that some parents got so nervous when their kids were on the ice that they actually left the arena. 1987 World Champion Brian Orser's mother was famous for it. She even left the stadium while her son was competing in the 1988 Olympic Games in their home country of Canada. Irina Slutskaya's mother never even travels with her daughter to competitions. She prefers to sit at home by the phone, biting her nails until Irina calls to say how she'd skated.

But Amy Hughes was having none of that.

"After what I went through last year, I'm going to watch," she told *The Daily News*.

"Mom didn't come this far to sit in the hallway," Sarah added.

And, what was more, Sarah was determined to make her mom happy she'd come.

To that end, thirteen-year-old Sarah Hughes stepped out onto the ice at the Delta Center in Salt Lake City with all the confidence of a veteran competitor.

Without any hesitation, she whipped off all seven elements of her two and a half minute short program, landing all of her jumps, hitting all of her spins, not letting a note of her music pass by.

It was the best performance she could have hoped for.

And it was good enough to put Sarah Hughes in second place after the Short Program. (As expected, Michelle Kwan was first.)

International Figure Skating Editor-in-Chief Lois Elfman wasn't surprised. "I knew the girls who were competing then. I had seen Sarah skate and I thought she could do really well."

Sarah, on the other hand, was stunned by the result.

At the press conference afterward, she pointed to Michelle Kwan and said, in wonderment, "It seems like a dream. I can't believe I'm sitting at a press table next to her."

She added, "It's so exciting. Last year I had so much fun and all the practices were so great and it was fun because there were always TV cameras everywhere and everybody wanting everybody's autograph. I'm so happy I'm here (this year). I'm happy that I skated well and I'm really pleased to be in second place."

With Sarah Hughes sitting in second place going into the Long Program, and another thirteen-year-old, Naomi Nari Nam, in fourth, the United States Figure Skating Association (USFSA) realized it might have a problem on their hands.

Traditionally, the top three girls from Nationals—the gold, silver, and bronze medal winners—were the ones sent to the World Championship to represent the U.S. But, the World Championship rules said that a girl had to be at least fifteen years old to compete. Both Sarah and Naomi were too young. Sarah knew all about the rule, which was why she could be so relaxed at Nationals. Since she thought she couldn't go, she wasn't worried about placing and making the World Team.

But, the USFSA was plenty worried.

*

AGAIN, Sarah Hughes waited.

Because she'd finished second in the Short Program, Sarah was scheduled to skate in the last group of girls for the Long Program. Fortunately, she didn't have to wait too long. She would be going first out of the last six girls. Sarah knew that if she won the Long Program she would win the entire event. The current leader, however, Michelle Kwan, would be skating after Sarah.

"Competing against Michelle is really exciting," Sarah

said in an ABC-TV interview. "Because she is one of my idols and I always watched her on TV and I've watched her competing at Worlds and I've watched her competing at Nationals before, and the Olympics and everything."

When Sarah took the ice to perform her Senior version of "Swan Lake" and compete for the first time against the girl she'd watched on television so many times, she was dressed in a white dress with a dipped neckline and short sleeves. Beads decorated the front of her dress, forming a V from her shoulders to the center to her chest. Her hair was up in a bun and held back with a matching scrunchie.

She set up her opening jump.

And then, the worst happened.

She fell.

"It's okay, it's okay," Sarah told herself, even as she continued skating, smiling, and pretending nothing had happened. She knew the worst thing she could do now was panic and lose her focus. If she lost her focus, Sarah would risk falling on everything.

"Don't think about the jump you missed," she lectured herself sternly. "Think about the jumps you still have to do."

She did her best. Right after the fall, Sarah landed her most difficult triple jump, the lutz, without a problem. But, later in the program, as she set up for her second lutz, the one she was supposed to do in combination with a double toe-loop, she stumbled, lost her balance, and again hit the ice with a smack.

Without dropping the smile from her face, Sarah

scrambled up and kept skating. It was imperative that she stay focused now, because coming up was a jump combination so difficult only one other skater, 1998 Olympic Champion Tara Lipinski, had ever landed it at the Nationals. A triple loop-triple loop.

In order to get full credit for it, Sarah would have to lift her left leg off the ice and, pushing off only from her right foot, jump in the air and turn three times, landing on the same right foot. Then, still without letting her left leg so much as brush the ice, Sarah would have to jump up again, turn three more times and, for the second time, land on her right foot, all the while keeping her balance, smiling, and making it look like it was the easiest thing in the world.

And she had to do all this after already falling on two jumps, including the one right before the combination.

Sarah concentrated all of her energy. And, in the space of a few seconds, she landed both jumps!

"When I did the triple loop-triple loop," she told the press later, "I was really happy because I did it right after I fell."

Still, no matter how pleased she was with the combination, when Sarah got off the ice, she knew she'd lost her chance to win the 1999 National Championship. Not that she'd ever really expected to do so. Still, sitting in second place after the Short Program, Sarah had honestly been hoping to leave Salt Lake City with at least a medal. But now, even that wasn't a sure thing.

"I've never competed in (Senior) Nationals before,"

Sarah said, "So this is a big step for me and I thought I performed okay."

But, would okay be good enough?

※
  ※
※ YES. And no. And yes, again.

Sarah's flawed skate wasn't good enough to keep her in second place. The silver medal instead, went to Naomi Nari Nam. It wasn't even good enough to keep Sarah in third. The bronze went to Angela Nikodinov.

At her first Senior Nationals, Sarah Hughes finished in fourth place. She did win a medal. It was the color pewter. The medal nobody really knew about.

Sensing that she was feeling less than happy with the result, Sarah's dad reassured her. He reminded the depressed teen how hard it was to win a medal at your first Senior National event, and hey, look at that, Sarah almost did it! She should be very, very proud of herself for how close she'd come.

Sarah figured he had a point. Besides, there really was no time to mope. Sarah knew that as soon as she got back home she'd need to start training for the Junior Grand Prix Final in March in Detroit. But, then, something amazing happened.

Naomi Nari Nam was too young to go to Worlds, which meant the USFSA would have to pick someone else, an alternate, to go in her place. Sarah figured she was out of the running. After all, she was thirteen, just like Naomi.

But, Sarah had something Naomi didn't. A silver medal from the Junior World Championships.

Sarah Hughes, striking just the right attitude, in her opening pose from her *Don Quixote* long program. (World Championships, Vancouver, B.C., March 2001)

© J. Barry Mittan

A twelve-year-old Sarah skating in her long program at the 1998 Junior National Championships in Philadelphia.

© Leah Adams

1998 Junior National champion Sarah Hughes on the podium with the other medalists: (from left to right) silver medalist Andrea Aggeler; Sarah; bronze medalist Erin Pearl; pewter medalist Naomi Nari Nam.

© Leah Adams

Sarah skating in the Exhibition after the competition at the 1998 National Championships.

© 1998 Kathy Goedeken

Sarah in a sit spin during the short program at the 1999 National Championships in Salt Lake City (her first senior competition).

© 1999 Kathy Goedeken

Sarah with her father, John Hughes, on the plane to Helsinki,
Finland, for the 1999 World Championships.

© Leah Adams

Sarah poses with the members of the U.S. World Team at the banquet at
the 1999 World Championships in Helsinki: (from left to right, top row)
Matthew Gates, Eve Chalom, Michael Weiss, Danielle Hartsell, Trifun
Zivanovic, Angela Nikodinov, John Zimmerman, Laura Handy, Timothy
Goebel, Peter Tchernyshev, Steve Hartsell. (Bottom row, left to right)
Michelle Kwan, Sarah, Naomi Lang.

© Leah Adams

Sarah with her coach, Robin
Wagner, at the press conference
after the 2000 Skate America held
in Colorado Springs.
© Leah Adams

Sarah performing her lon
program to *Turandot* at the 200
National Championships i
Clevelan
© 2000 Kathy Goedek

Sarah unveils a sassy, provocative side
with her new exhibition/interpretative
free program to selections from the
musical *Fosse*. The program is full of atti
tude and classic Fosse dance moves,
which she performed with confidence
and flair. (Exhibition, 2001 World
Championships, Vancouver, B.C.)
© J. Barry Mittan

Sarah with her coach and four-time world champion Kurt Browning at a practice for the 2000 Hershey Kisses Pro-Am.

© 2000 Kathy Goedeken

Sarah with Robin Wagner in the "kiss & cry" area after Sarah's long program at the 2001 National Championships in Boston. Sarah and Robin are justifiably thrilled with her marks.

© 2001 Kathy Goedeken

Sarah signing autographs after winning the silver medal at the 2001 National Championships. In only a couple of years, Sarah has gained many devoted fans.

© 2001 Kathy Goedeken

Sarah in her classic layback spin during the short program to *Vocalise* at the 2001 World Championships in Vancouver. Her position is absolutely exquisite.

© Leah Adams

Sarah performing a gorgeous forward inside spiral during her long program at the 2001 World Championships.

© J. Barry Mittan

Sarah in mid-air during one of the difficult jumps in her long program at the 2001 World Championships.
© 2001 Kathy Goedeken

Sarah on the awards podium with gold medalist Michelle Kwan (center) and silver medalist Irina Slutskaya (left) at the 2001 World Championships.
© Leah Adams

2001 World bronze medalist Sarah Hughes.

The World Championship rules said that a skater had to be at least fifteen years old to compete. *Unless* she also had a medal from that year's Junior World Championship.

Sarah Hughes may have been two years too young, but she was going to Helsinki!

How cool is that? Sarah thought when she found out she could go. The whole year, she thought that even if she medaled at Nationals, she couldn't go to Worlds. It never even crossed her mind that she might be eligible to go to Worlds as a result of her Junior Worlds medal!

And if Sarah thought a trip to Helsinki would be "cool," both of her parents were blown away by the development.

Sarah's dad had been thrilled with her fourth-place finish. To think that she also qualified for the World Team was simply incredible.

Her mom had an even more emotional reaction, exclaiming to *The Great Neck Record*, "I still can't believe that Sarah will be competing at the World Championship. I know she's good, but she's only thirteen!"

AT thirteen, Sarah Hughes was the youngest girl in the entire World Championship competition. Most of the other young women were in their late teens, like the American favorite, Michelle Kwan. Two top-seeded skaters, Russia's Maria Butyrskaya and Kazakhstan's Tatiana Malinina were twenty-six and twenty-seven, more than twice Sarah's age.

But Sarah refused to let the fact that the World Championship would be her first ever international Senior competition bother or intimidate her. She didn't even really think about it. She just wanted to show that she could do well, and that, just like Robin had reminded her about Nationals, she belonged. Sarah knew that she was in Helsinki to do a job, and she was determined to do the best she could.

To that end, even though she was in ninth place after the Short Program and knew there was virtually no chance of winning a medal, Sarah skated her long program like a champion, landing all of her jumps, including the pesky second triple lutz that had tripped her up at the Nationals.

Getting off the ice, Sarah told the press, "I'm just happy that I skated as well as I did. I was pretty nervous today, because I did all the events here, and it's a little tiring. I was having so much fun. Making the World Team was one of the high points of the season for me. The competition itself was really thrilling. I was so proud to be representing my country and to be skating so well. I think that I didn't feel as much pressure as I did at Nationals. At Nationals, I was holding back and at Worlds, I felt much better and my head was all there."

Not only was Sarah's head all there, but her marks were, too. Her flawless long program moved her up to seventh place. At only thirteen years old, Sarah Hughes was ranked in the top ten in the World. (Her hero, Michelle Kwan, had only finished eighth at *her* first World Championship, in 1994; and the reigning Olympic Champion, Tara Lipinski was fifteenth!)

As for Robin, she thought being at Worlds was a great opportunity for Sarah. Her student got to be on the ice with the best of the best, and she'd gotten a chance to show how she had enhanced her skating and grown as a person. They couldn't have written it any better.

Sarah's long, drawn-out season (which, between Nationals and Worlds also included a silver medal at the Junior Grand Prix Final) was finally over. It had proven successful beyond anyone's wildest dreams. It even added a new superstition to Sarah's life.

"I have so many superstitions," Sarah revealed to US Olympicteam.com, "it's not even funny. If I do something before I skate and I skate well, I just add it to my list. (After Worlds) I've been wearing the same pajamas the night before I skate. But, I'm not to the point where I don't wash the pajamas."

Sarah's season may have been over, but her life as a world-class skater was just beginning.

THE Fall of 1999 promised to bring a lot of changes to Sarah's everyday life. 1999–2000 would be her first season as a full-time Senior competitor. She was scheduled to compete in an open international (a competition of professionals and amateurs) in Canada, her dad's home country. She was scheduled to compete in Florida. In Vienna, Austria. In Paris, France. And all of those were *before* the 2000 National Championships in Cleveland, where Sarah once again was hoping to skate well enough to make the World team and travel to Nice on the French Riviera.

Oh, and one more thing. In the fall of 1999, Sarah Hughes started her freshman year of high school.

Right away, she knew that a typical schedule would be out of the question. But, Sarah was used to the drill by now. Even back in first grade she'd had to balance school with skating. Her mom remembers that both Sarah and little sister Emily were fortunate enough to have Ms. Pat Master as their first-grade teacher. Ms. Master encouraged them to pursue the activities they loved, but also to keep up with their studies.

Sarah took her teacher's words to heart while she was still in grammar school, and later, when she was in middle school, too. Sarah says that in middle school the teachers continued to be kind to her and to understand about the traveling she had to do for competitions. Now that she's in high school, some teachers even come to her house to give her work to complete while she's on the road at competitions. And when she comes back they're there to help her or explain things. Sarah's teachers also schedule make-up tests for her, and allow Sarah to leave school early or come in late, as her schedule demands.

The entire Hughes family is very grateful for the accommodation. Sarah's mother has even publicly thanked the faculty of North Middle School for being so cooperative and understanding.

Robin is grateful, too. She told *Blades on Ice Magazine*, "The school is wonderful about working with her schedule and keeping her in school."

Thanks to her success in middle school, her freshman

year Sarah signed up for all Honors classes at Great Neck High School. That same year, she soon won the Presidential Award for Academic Excellence.

Her father thinks that one of the reasons Sarah gets such good grades is because she wants to perform well at whatever she does. To her, grades are the same as the scores judges give out after a performance. Grades are just another competition. And Sarah is a tough competitor. She plays to win.

Yet, even in spite of all the extra help she receives, due to Sarah's complicated schedule and long commute, she manages to attend only one class a day at her high school. She does the rest of the work either on her own or with a tutor. Some critics have wondered why she bothers showing up at all. Why not be like most skaters and do all of her work through correspondence courses and home schooling?

Sarah's dad won't hear of it. While he doesn't fault anyone for home schooling or employing full-time tutors, the Hughes family believes that education isn't just about memorizing facts. It's about learning in a group and especially about hanging out with peers and friends.

Sarah agrees. Friends are her most important reason for going to school, even if it's only one class a day and even if it makes her schedule even crazier.

"Sometimes school can be really, really stressful," she admitted to Cleveland.com. "Like if I have to do an essay. But, I really like math and science and I like being able to go to school. When I come back from competitions, kids will say, 'Oh, we saw you on TV and we were all cheering for you.' I feel a whole support system from my school, and that's really nice. I have the best of both worlds. Some kids think it's cool that I've been to Paris. And now that some people have seen me on TV, I'm Sarah the Skater. When TV crews come to school, everybody starts crowding around me. I suddenly have more lab partners. But, I enjoy being the center of attention. And I can always find someone if I want to hang out."

As far as Sarah's mom is concerned, her daughter has a very balanced life, made up of equal parts friends, school, skating and hobbies (Sarah plays the violin, though, she admits, not very well.) Sure, it's busier and more hectic than the average teen's, but her mom thinks that Sarah has shown she can handle it.

In 1999, though, it was time to find out if she could both handle it, and the pressure that comes with Senior international competition.

CHAPTER EIGHT

The Competition: U.S.

JUST because Sarah Hughes has proven herself in Senior National competition for three straight years is no guarantee that she will automatically win a medal at the 2002 Nationals or be guaranteed a spot on the 2002 Olympic team.

The United States Ladies' field is extremely deep, and with only three slots available, all the girls are expected to fight tooth and nail for each Olympic berth.

To begin with, even not counting Michelle Kwan, who, barring a true tragedy, is the only one honestly guaranteed a spot on the Olympic team, there will probably still be three women at the National Championships who have all beaten Sarah before in competition.

One of them is Angela Nikodinov, who was third in 1999 to Sarah's fourth. In January of 2002, Angela will be twenty-two years old, and a seasoned competitor. To put things in perspective, in 1994, when Sarah was barely nine years old, Angela was already the fifth-ranked Junior skater in the country. And, in 1997, when Sarah was still struggling to qualify out of her section as a Novice skater, Angela was ranked number four as a Senior at Nationals.

A year later, in 1998, Angela was fifth at Nationals, but after both Tara Lipinski, the 1998 U.S. silver medalist, and Nicole Bobek, the 1998 U.S. bronze medalist, declined to go to the World Championship, Angela was named to the World team.

Unfortunately, Angela was nowhere to be found.

Thinking that her season was over, Angela and her parents took off for a vacation in her folks' home country of Bulgaria without leaving their contact information with the USFSA. After all, Angela's chances of being called up were practically nonexistent. She wasn't even the first alternate—that was fourth-place finisher Tonia Kwiatkowski. Angela was the second alternate. And nobody could remember the last time a second alternate had made it to Worlds. So the Nikodinovs figured they were in the clear. They left the country. And, as a result, Angela missed her chance to compete at her first World Championships.

For a skater who'd worked her entire life to be named to the U.S. World Team, the near-miss had to be devastating.

Which was why, the following year in 1999, she returned to Nationals with a new dedication and determination to make the World Team—for real, this time, none of that alternate stuff.

She skated well. Not her best ever, but, good enough for a third-place finish. In 1999, Angela Nikodinov would be going to the World Championships not as a second string replacement, but as the number two girl on the U.S. team. (Because Silver Medalist Naomi Nari Nam was too young to qualify for the Worlds, Angela's bronze medal was still enough to make her the number two girl. The number three girl, Sarah Hughes, had placed fourth.)

At the 1999 Worlds, Angela skated far from her best, placing twelfth and ending up behind Sarah Hughes, whom Angela had beaten only a few weeks before. It was an unusual turn of events, but not an unprecedented one. After all, only a year earlier, Michelle Kwan came in second to Tara Lipinski at the Olympics after decisively beating her at the Nationals only a month before.

Still, it's never fun to place behind a girl you expected to beat.

Unfortunately for Angela, the trend would continue through 2000. At the 2000 Nationals, she dropped back down to fourth. This time, Sarah was third. Once again, because Silver Medalist Sasha Cohen was too young to travel to the World Championships, Angela got to go in her place. This time, she placed ninth. Finally in the top ten.

And, at the 2001 Nationals, a new Angela seemed to emerge. She skated better than anyone had ever seen her do. She was sharp and she was graceful and she was *on*. She fought her way back onto the podium, finishing third at the Nationals, second at the international Four Continents Championships, and fifth at the 2001 World Championships.

In one season, Angela Nikodinov declared herself a contender for a medal at the 2002 Olympics.

If she succeeds, she will, at the ripe old age of almost twenty-two, be considered one of the "older" women of skating. And in a way she is—considering that two of the girls Michelle Kwan, Sarah Hughes, and Angela Nikodinov will be doing battle with at the 2002 U.S. Nationals very well might be sixteen-year-old Naomi Nari Nam and seventeen-year-old Sasha Cohen.

Both are onetime U.S. silver medalists, but both have also struggled with injuries since winning their medals.

Naomi placed a surprise second at the 1999 Nationals. But in 2000, her growing body made all those jumps that had once come so easily feel difficult and awkward (what Russia's Maria Butyrskaya once predicted about her rival, Irina Slutskaya). Naomi made mistake after mistake in both the Short Program and the Long, finishing a very disappointing eighth. Then, in 2001, various injuries kept her from competing at all.

If Naomi, who lists "becoming Olympic champion" as the number one goal on her USFSA bio, intends to secure herself a spot on the 2002 Olympic team, she's going to have to work harder and pull off the skate of her life at the 2002 Nationals.

The same holds true for her training and rink mate, Sasha Cohen. Sasha and Naomi both skate in Costa Mesa, California, with coach John Nicks, coincidently Angela Nikodinov's former coach, as well.

In 1999, while Naomi was making a big splash in Senior Ladies with her surprise silver medal, Sasha was winning a silver medal of her own—in the Junior division.

However, a year later, it was Sasha who was cradling the 2000 Senior silver, having beaten not only Naomi, but Sarah Hughes as well.

Fans of both skaters were looking forward to a Sarah/Sasha rematch at the 2001 Nationals, but it wasn't to be. Like Naomi, Sasha withdrew from those Nationals due to injuries. But, she swore she'd be back to challenge for a spot on the 2002 Olympic team.

She, along with Naomi and 2000 World Junior Champion Jennifer Kirk and 2001 World Junior Silver Medalist Ann Patrice McDonough, will all be part of the "teen" invasion, the "kids" everyone talks about, the ones who are poised to try and dethrone reigning champion Michelle Kwan at the 2002 Nationals.

What's funny, though, is when experts talk about "the kids," they rarely mention another kid, Sarah Hughes.

After all, in January of 2002, Sarah herself will only be sixteen years old (she was born on May 2, 1985). She's actually younger than Sasha Cohen and Jenny Kirk, and almost exactly the same age as Ann Patrice McDonough.

But somehow, Sarah just isn't a "kid."

Maybe the key difference between Sarah and the other girls is that Sarah looks her age, and the others don't. They look younger than they are, and so they look precocious and advanced. And they look cute. Sometimes cute can count for a lot.

Or maybe the reason the other girls seem younger than Sarah is simply because she's been around the skating scene for so much longer. The other girls are called the young up-and-comers because they're new. While Sarah is, to a certain point, taken for granted. She's been an international competitor for so long that everyone simply assumes she's got to be older than Sasha and Naomi and Jenny and Ann Patrice.

They forget that, at her first Senior international competition, Sarah Hughes was all of thirteen years old.

And that she's still just a high schooler, albeit one with very big dreams, and an even bigger talent.

CHAPTER NINE

Making the Grade

SARAH Hughes began her first full season as a Senior Ladies international competitor at the Grand Slam of Skating, an open international event in Kitchner, Ontario. Since Sarah's dad, John, grew up in Scarborough, Canada, a supportive group of Sarah's relatives turned up to watch her skate.

An open international is different from a regular, qualifying competition in that the skaters are often asked to skate an "interpretive free" program. A program that's judged not just on jumps and spins and other such technical elements, but also on how well the skater feels and interprets their music. It is a program judged more on emotion than on hard, objective criteria.

An interpretive free program, like an exhibition, is supposed to be dramatic or sexy or fun or even goofy. Most of all, it should be memorable and distinctive.

For her first interpretative artistic program, Sarah and Robin put together a Beatles medley number.

"Both Robin and I like the Beatles," Sarah told *Blades on Ice*. "And we wanted a number with both fast and slow tempos."

Although Sarah placed fourth in the women's event, because this was a "team" competition (skaters were grouped into pairs and their scores combined), she and her partner, Russia's Evgeny Plushenko, managed to finish first overall.

"I think it's cool," Sarah said about her teammate at a press conference after the event, "Because he's the youngest guy and I'm the youngest girl."

Although, lest anyone think that Sarah was dissing some of the older skaters at the event, she added, "It's just an honor to be here skating with such great skaters, with World and Olympic champions. I didn't really feel like I was competing against [two-time Olympic Gold Medalist] Katarina Witt. I felt more like I was skating with her."

After Canada, Sarah stopped briefly in Orlando, Florida, to compete in the Keri Lotion Figure Skating Classic, where she placed sixth, then hopped directly onto a plane for Austria and the Vienna Cup.

While in Vienna, Sarah got a special treat: Tickets to see the Vienna State Opera House perform Giacomo Puccini's *Turandot*. Sarah would be skating to excerpts from this opera, including the most famous part, "Nessum Dorma," her 1999–2000 season long program.

Robin told *Blades on Ice*, "I found their schedule on the Internet and couldn't believe the wonderful timing. Sarah will be able to see others performing (to her music), see the costumes, the expressions and emotions."

But, even though she thought it would be a wonderful experience for Sarah to see her music interpreted by professional singers and performers, Robin didn't intend for Sarah to portray the melodramatic story in her free skating. For one thing, it was just too bloody.

Turandot, while written by the Italian Puccini, is set in ancient China, where the vengeful Princess Turandot has decreed that anyone seeking her hand in marriage must answer three riddles or die. Many princes have tried, failed, and been summarily executed, their heads displayed before the crowd. Calaf, a foreign prince in disguise, is struck by Turandot's beauty and resolves to win her. But, when Calaf answers the three riddles successfully, Turandot refuses to marry him as promised. Calaf then offers to die if Turandot can guess his name by the next morning. That night, Turandot sends her troops throughout Peking to discover Calaf's name. In the morning, Turandot and Calaf confront each other. Calaf declares his love, and forces a kiss on her. Turandot melts, and Calaf reveals his name. Turandot summons her court and declares she has learned the stranger's name—it is "Love."

While *Turandot* is unquestionably a powerful and romantic story, Robin nevertheless thought that its themes of torture, obsession, and death were too complex, and that Sarah, at age fourteen, was too young to tackle them.

So, instead, Robin and Sarah adapted the opera's story to something more age appropriate. Instead of the specific saga of Turandot and Calaf, they decided that Sarah would merely portray a Chinese princess with many suitors vying for her hand.

It was simpler that way, and more fitting for a young girl.

After Vienna, where she finished first, Sarah returned to the United States and her first Grand Prix event, Skate America. (Like the Junior Grand Prix, the Senior Grand Prix is also a series of point earning competitions, with a final at the end.)

Sarah was particularly excited to be making her Grand Prix debut in her home country. She told *Blades on Ice*, "This is my first Senior Grand Prix event. It's great since it's in America. I feel very comfortable here. Worlds last year helped me feel like I fit in with these other skaters. I used to watch it on TV and I'm thrilled I'll get to skate here."

Along with two brand-new programs, the *Turandot* long and a German movie sound track, *Klara*, for her short, Sarah also had a pair of brand-new costumes for the season. For her short program she was wearing a sleeveless light blue costume Robin described as "Romeo and Juliet style," with an empire waist, and a longer skirt than what Sarah had worn in the past. Robin thinks it's really important that Sarah, at her age, be very comfortable with her costume and love what she's wearing.

Sarah's costume for the Long Program was also blue,

but a more royal shade, with lace and beading, long, snug sleeves and a mandarin collar. She was, after all, portraying a lovely princess.

Sarah didn't skate her best at Skate America. Her programs were still new and she was struggling to get used to them. But, nevertheless, she placed fourth overall (and second in the Short Program) behind Michelle Kwan, and Russia's Julia Soldatova and Elena Sokolova. Pretty impressive considering that Michelle and Elena were former Olympians and Julia a World Junior Champion.

Sarah's second Grand Prix of the season, Trophee Lalique in Paris, went much smoother. She placed third behind reigning World Champion Maria Butyrskaya and Viktoria Volchkova, the girl Sarah beat at the Junior World Championships a year earlier.

Sarah told the press, "I'm really happy with how I skated. I went out there very determined because I knew I was prepared."

Something else Sarah felt prepared for was all the shopping she and her mom did while in Paris. Now that Amy Hughes was fully recovered, she and her daughter had a lot of missed store-hopping time to make up for!

HARD as it may have been to believe, even with all of the traveling that she did that season, Sarah still didn't skate in all of the events she'd been invited to.

Robin explained that she and the Hugheses have tried not to take everything that Sarah was offered because they believed some downtime between events was important.

Not to mention training time for the more important competitions, like the 2000 U.S. Nationals, held that year in Cleveland, Ohio.

Sarah was very eager to make the World team again, though she knew that just because she'd done it last year was no guarantee it would happen again. If she got to make the trip to Nice, France, Sarah would have to earn it, just like anyone else.

To that end, Sarah trained her very hardest. Rather than just practicing her program once from beginning to end with all of the jumps and spins, Sarah ran through her programs twice, back to back, hoping to increase her stamina and mental toughness. If Sarah could land all of her jumps the second time around, even when her legs felt like jelly and she thought she might collapse from exhaustion, it would give her confidence that she'd be able to land them under pressure, when it really counted.

She also polished her presentation skills, finishing her line, paying more attention to detail. And she worked more on her spiral, doing lots of stretching exercises daily.

A spiral is one of the few skating moves that's neither a jump nor a spin nor a footwork sequence. A spiral requires skating forward on one foot, arms gracefully outstretched, while the other leg is raised as high as possible. Some skaters, like 1995 U.S. Champion Nicole Bobek, can raise their free leg so high, it's almost perpendicular to the ice. Other skaters, like Michelle Kwan and Sasha Cohen, do what's known as a Charlotte Spiral. They raise one leg behind them and bend over until their hands can touch the foot that's on the ice, and their faces are pressed into their knees.

A spiral is one of those moves that makes a skater look flexible and graceful. When Robin is working with Sarah on a spiral, she often skates right behind her, and as Sarah stretches her arms and her legs as far as she possibly can, Robin calls out to her, urging her to stretch even more than that. She tells Sarah to imagine herself being beautiful and graceful and of letting the music lift her until she's practically floating on the very, very edge of her blade.

Heading into the 2000 Nationals, Robin described their game plan to *International Figure Skating Magazine* this way: "We will continue to work on (Sarah's) speed and her posture, and just taking her overall skating to a higher level. Basically, we'll just be paying a lot of attention to everything."

They would have to. Because this year, unlike the last, Robin knew that everyone would be paying attention to Sarah. In only one short year, she'd gone from being just another Junior skater to the girl some people believed had a chance to beat Michelle Kwan.

There were a couple of reasons for that. For one thing, Michelle hadn't been skating as well during the 1999–2000 season as she had in the past. The nineteen-year-old had started classes at UCLA in the fall, and suddenly seemed to be having a bit of trouble juggling school and skating.

She told *Newsday* that after having been privately tutored since eighth grade, "When I walked into that UCLA lecture hall, I felt so small. I felt like an ant, so out of place."

Not the best feeling with which to then turn around and try to take on the world.

Although she'd won both of her Grand Prix events, Skate America and Skate Canada, Michelle finished second at the Grand Prix final in Lyon, France, to Russia's Irina Slutskaya. Coming into Nationals, the buzz among skating fans and self-proclaimed pundits was that Michelle wasn't challenging herself technically. She'd struggled with landing a triple-triple combination all season, while Irina was regularly landing triple-triple combinations, including two in one program at the Grand Prix Final.

At the 2000 Nationals, Sarah Hughes was planning to do the same thing.

After all, if Irina Slutskaya and 1998 Olympic Champion Tara Lipinski were able to beat Michelle's superior, polished, experienced artistry by pushing the technical stakes and whipping out the triple-triples, why shouldn't Sarah Hughes give it a shot?

Even though she knew it was a major risk. A fall on such a difficult maneuver could drop Sarah right off the podium. Many thought she should play it safe, skate a conservative, easier program, stay upright, and protect her hard-won National ranking.

But, as Sarah told Cleveland.com, "If I can do the triple-triples then I should do them. I don't want to fall behind. I want to be right on them. If I don't, I'll never know how good I can be."

In 2000, Sarah was even more excited about Nationals than she had been the previous year—if such a thing were possible. Being fourteen, she naturally tried to play it cool, pretend it wasn't such a big deal, just another competition. But, inside, she was dying to get to Cleveland. Her goals were simple and clear. She wanted to win a medal. She wanted to stand on the podium and wave to the crowd. But, more than anything, she wanted to skate well. After her two falls last year, Sarah was dying to show the world what she could really do.

Though the thing about skating is, when it comes to winning a championship, just showing the world what you could do in competition isn't enough. First, you had to show them what you could do in the practice.

It may be hard for the casual figure skating fan who only watches the event on television to understand, but judges don't just judge on what is put in front of them on the ice. They judge the practices, too. The judges picked to work a given event (like Ladies' Singles, or Men's, or Pairs), come to the practices and take careful notes on what everyone is working on. As they watch a skater struggle with their triple lutz, or effortlessly twirl through a difficult combination spin, they estimate what kind of scores they'll be giving this skater in the actual competition. They set a "base mark" for the elements, then deduct accordingly if the skater stumbles on the move during actual competition. As publisher Mark Lund explained in *International Figure Skating Magazine*, "The judges have to watch the practices. They must get an understanding of who is doing what and how they, in all likelihood, are going to perform."

That's why it's imperative to be perfect in the practices, too.

And, in 2000, with a year of international competitive experience under her belt, Sarah Hughes was more than ready for the challenge.

As soon as she got to Nationals, she checked in, got her picture taken for the competitors I.D. badge, and received her competition booklet, telling Sarah what practice group she would be in and when her practice times were. Practices at Nationals weren't like the two-hour sessions she was used to back home. Most of the time, they were only about half an hour long. Just long enough to keep in shape and do your program for the judges. Not long enough to really learn anything new.

Still, there is nothing like a practice session at a major competition. Especially that first practice session, when the day is still new, no one has skated yet, and every girl has, theoretically, as much of a chance of winning as the next one.

For that first practice session, the ice has been freshly cleaned. The only marks on it are from the Zamboni's tires, not from skates, and a white fog hangs over it like a cloud. Most of the arena seats are empty. Only the hard-core fans are there, and they sit quietly, respectfully, clapping for their favorites, but not so loudly as to disturb the others. A handful of coaches stand by the boards, each one whispering instructions and encouragement to their own skaters, their voices echoing like in a cave and bouncing off the scoreboards. There's tension in the air, and nerves and butterflies in the stomach. But also excitement. Anticipation. And, above all, hope.

Maybe this year, the air seems to whisper. Maybe this is my time, my season, my chance. On the first practice session of a major competition, anything is possible.

Especially when you're fourteen years old and already a World competitor and you know your whole family is in Cleveland, ready, willing and able to cheer you on. They're here for you if you succeed. They're here for you if you fail. And, no matter what happens, you know that after all the medals have been handed out and the pictures taken, you've still got homework to do back in your hotel room. Because no matter how helpful Sarah's teachers were about giving her time off from school to attend the Nationals, there was still homework to be handed in when she got back. In every subject.

Though Sarah actually attends class for biology and history, she has a tutor for English and math, and, like she told *Newsday*: "That's harder than being in class. Because when it's just you and the teacher, you sort of have to do your work."

SARAH Hughes waited.

There is no qualifying routine at the National Championships. Up first is the Short Program. The skaters pick their "skate order," the order in which they'll take the ice, by picking a number out of a hat. Popular wisdom says that the later you go, the better. Popular wisdom says that judges "save" their marks, that they don't give out any numbers that are too high to early skaters because, if they did that, what would they give if someone else then came out and skated even better? Popular wisdom says it's good to skate toward the end.

But it also means a lot of waiting.

At the 2000 Nationals, Sarah Hughes drew to skate after last year's Silver Medalist Naomi Nari Nam. After Angela Nikodinov. After Amber Corwin. After Michelle Kwan.

So Sarah Hughes waited.

She didn't watch her competitors. What would be the point, after all? How the other girls skated wouldn't change what Sarah was planning to do on the ice. The Short Program was all required elements. It's not like Sarah could suddenly improvise a new jump or a new spin into her program. The only thing watching the other girls could do was make Sarah nervous. Why risk it?

So, while her competitors took the ice one by one, Sarah stayed in the back of the arena, in the warm-up area, stretching, listening to music, getting last minute advice from Robin.

And missing the drama taking place outside.

First, Naomi Nari Nam, struggling with a maturing body and a season of injuries, made three major mistakes, effectively taking herself out of the running for the gold medal.

And then, most shocking of all, Michelle Kwan took a spill, falling on one of her easier jumps, the triple toe loop.

Sarah wasn't watching the competition. But, there was no missing the loud "Oh!" that exploded from the crowd, loud enough to rattle the building, as soon as Michelle fell.

Even backstage, Sarah heard them gasp in shock. And she'd been to enough skating events to know what the sound meant.

Still, even with that one major mistake on a required element, Michelle was in first place.

Up next was Angela Nikodinov, who skated cleanly, but was judged not good enough to move ahead of Michelle.

And then came Sasha Cohen.

A year older than Sarah, but several inches tinier. At four feet nine inches tall, and seventy-nine pounds, Sasha looked like a delicate ten-year-old. And she skated like a prima ballerina.

To the surprise of everyone who'd never even heard of last year's Junior National Silver Medalist, Sasha Cohen skated a flawless short program, complete with triple jumps, beautiful spins, a Charlotte spiral, and graceful movements that brought to mind classical skaters like Peggy Fleming or Ekaterina Gordeeva.

Sarah wasn't watching Sasha skate. But, just like with the gasp of horror that Michelle got, she heard the crowd explode into wild cheers and applause. They got up on their feet, they threw teddy bears and flowers onto the ice, they gave the Southern California pixie the first standing ovation of the night. And, when the scoreboard showed Sasha ahead of Michelle, the crowd roared their enthusiasm.

Now, Sarah Hughes had to go out there and follow Sasha's perfect performance.

Sensing that her prize pupil might feel a bit intimidated, Robin grabbed Sarah for a quick pep talk. Practically willing her to keep it together and not get distracted, Robin urged Sarah to go out there and show the crowd just how terrific she was.

And yet, even though she might have been a bit rattled, Robin wasn't ever truly worried. She told *Newsday*, after the event, "I could see in Sarah's demeanor that she was ready. She's had nice practices, both here and at home before we came. I felt a certain calm in watching her skate. I just really enjoyed it."

And Sarah did not disappoint.

Despite having to follow the most popular new star of the night, she knocked off all of her elements one by one, just the way she and Robin had practiced them endless times. She was crisp, she was sharp, and she was on. It may not have been the greatest performance Sarah ever skated. But, it was enough to put her in second place behind Sasha Cohen. And ahead of Michelle Kwan.

At the press conference afterward, Sarah admitted, "It's not easy to go out after a standing ovation. But, I just tried to stay focused and I'm very pleased with the way I skated."

And Michelle Kwan had a confession of her own to make. Sitting at a table in front of several dozen journalists, she pointed to Sasha and Sarah and admitted, "I do see the future. I was watching them skate and I see great potential."

Nevertheless, Sarah and Sasha were sitting in very different boats. Sasha's situation was closer to the situation

Sarah had been in the previous year. She was new, she was unknown, and, although a year older than Sarah, she was considered one of the young guns. Still, standing ovation or no standing ovation, Sarah wouldn't have traded places with Sasha at that moment for anything in the world.

As Robin told *International Figure Skating Magazine*, "The pressure of the unknown (as with last year's Senior debut) is more difficult for Sarah to deal with. The pressure of expectation is something that we speak about, we analyze, and we separate from our expectations. Therefore, in the long run, that's an easier pressure for her to deal with."

But, that was the long run.

In the short run, Sarah had a chance to become the new National Champion. She, as well as practically everyone in the audience, knew that whichever one of the top three girls, Sasha, Sarah, or Michelle, won the Long Program, would win the title as well.

At the same press conference, Robin stated the obvious when she admitted that she was much happier with Sarah sitting behind the unranked Sasha than three-time National Champion Michelle.

If it came down to a head to head, Sasha, Robin presumed, would be easier for Sarah to take than Michelle.

For the Long Program, the top six girls would skate in the last group. Sarah drew to skate first of the six.

To some, this would have been a problem. Not only is it part of the belief that the later you go the higher your marks are likely to be, there is also the warm-up factor. Prior to skating their programs, all the skaters in one group are given several minutes of warm-up time. Obviously, the skater set to compete first can't use every moment of the warm-up and risk being too tired for the actual performance. So, those scheduled to skate first usually only try a jump and spin or two, then skate over to the barrier and just wait.

So, once again, Sarah Hughes waited.

And she insisted to *Newsday*: "I like to go first. I'm all warmed up and I can just go."

And go she did.

Wearing the dark blue dress with sparkling crystals sewn into a shimmering pattern, her hair pulled back into a bun, Sarah took the ice at her second Senior National Championship.

Even before she'd started skating, ABC-TV commentator and 1968 Olympic Champion Peggy Fleming was raving, "In just twelve short months, Sarah has changed from that awkward thirteen-year-old girl we first saw and now she is a poised and elegant competitor."

Sarah's first planned jump was a double axel—a forward take off, then two and a half revolutions in the air, landing on the right foot. She nailed it.

"Very light, very easy," praised ABC commentator and two-time Olympic Gold Medalist Dick Button.

Up next was the first of two triple-triple combinations Sarah had planned: A triple salchow-triple loop.

Once again, Sarah landed both jumps, completing six revolutions in less than ten seconds.

In less than ten seconds, Sarah had made history. Not

only was it the first time she'd landed the combination in competition, it was also the first time that combination had ever been landed at the United States Nationals!

But, there was no time to rest on her laurels. After only a combination spin during which to catch her breath, Sarah still had another triple-triple combination to do.

A triple toe–triple loop.

To the audience, it looked as if the triple toe was done without any problems. But, Sarah felt off-balance, her timing was off, something didn't feel right.

And so, as she went up to do her triple loop, Sarah "popped" the jump. She opened up her arms too early, which stopped her rotation in the air. Instead of the triple she'd been planning on, Sarah only landed a single loop.

Once again, however, Sarah refused to allow the mistake to rattle her concentration. As she told *Newsday*, later, "You know, you can't freak out when you miss something. The performance goes on. I knew I could do everything else, and you can't go back and change what you didn't do."

So, rather than dwelling on what she couldn't change, Sarah focused on the jumps she still had to land and the spins she still had to complete.

A triple lutz. Good. Then a layback spin.

"Perfect position," Peggy Fleming raved. "Wonderful arch in her back."

Triple flip. Another double axel. Triple salchow.

Another fall!

Sarah felt her chance at the gold medal slipping away.

Still, she got up and kept going. She forced herself not to think about what had just happened.

There was only one move left, a combination sit-spin.

"An almost perfect program," Dick Button proclaimed.

But, not the program Sarah had hoped for.

She glided off the ice. There was nothing left for her to do now but wait for the other girls to finish skating, and wait for the judges to rank them all. Wait to find out if this year, she'd managed to hold on to second place, or maybe, maybe even win the whole thing.

But, again, it was not to be. Even though they both also fell, Michelle Kwan went on to win her fourth National title, while Sasha Cohen dropped down one place to take second. Sarah Hughes placed third.

She'd gotten the medal she so wanted before coming to Cleveland.

And this year, there were no loopholes necessary to place Sarah on the U.S. team for the World Championships in Nice, France.

She'd earned her spot.

Now, it was time to take on the world.

But, first, there was something very, very important Sarah still needed to take care of.

CHAPTER TEN

The Competition: Michelle Kwan

*

* It seems like at every Nationals, as she steps in front of the pool of reporters there to cover the latest championship, Sarah is asked the same question: Can you beat Michelle?

It's all anyone wants to know: Sarah, can you beat Michelle Kwan?

To Sarah, it feels like the press is desperate to stir up a rivalry and make their stories more interesting. They want to write that Sarah and Michelle hate each other. They want to write that Sarah stays up nights biting her nails and saying her prayers and wishing for Michelle to fall down and break a leg. They seem kind of disappointed when they find out that isn't the case.

To be honest, Sarah doesn't quite understand what all the fuss is about. And so she ends up giving more or less the same answer each and every time she hears the question.

"Every skater wants to win and I want to win," she confesses. "But when I go out there, I'm trying to beat myself and if I beat other people with my skating, great."

But, on the other hand, there are "other people," and then there's Michelle Kwan.

No other woman has dominated U.S. women's skating to the extent that this four-time World Champion has.

Before Michelle, for the last twenty years, the Ladies' U.S. title tended to be passed back and forth among a small group of girls. Elaine Zayak won the National title in 1981, and then Rosalynn Sumners won it for the next three years. Tiffany Chin in 1985. Debi Thomas in 1986. Jill Trenary in 1987. Debi Thomas in 1988. Jill Trenary in 1989 and 1990. Tonya Harding in 1991. Kristi Yamaguchi in 1992. Nancy Kerrigan in 1993. Tonya Harding in 1994 (though she would later lose the title for her role in Nancy's injury). Nicole Bobek in 1995.

And then came Michelle Kwan.

She won the title in 1996. (Losing it to Tara Lipinski in 1997.) In 1998. In 1999. In 2000. And in 2001.

She is the first woman to win four consecutive National titles since Linda Fratianne (1977–1980). And the first one to win five in total since Janet Lynn (1969–1973). If Michelle, as expected, wins another National title in 2002, she will have more U.S. titles than Dorothy Hamill, who won only three. And Peggy Fleming, who won five.

She will be, like she's always said she wanted to be, a legend.

But, even legends are fallible. Despite her sterling record, Michelle has not won every competition she's ever entered, or even every competition that she was favored to win.

In 1995, Michelle Kwan, the 1994 U.S. silver medalist, was heavily favored to win the National title. She came in second to Nicole Bobek.

In 1997, the reigning U.S. and World Champion was expected to repeat in both. She lost both to Tara Lipinski.

In 1998, U.S. Champion Michelle was expected to win the Olympics. She didn't.

In 1999, she was expected to win the World Championship. She didn't.

On the other hand, in 2000 and 2001, Michelle entered Worlds as the underdog, and, both times, she whipped out a pair of brilliant programs to decisively and inarguably win the entire thing.

Michelle Kwan can never be counted out.

And she can never be counted in.

She is the ultimate question mark at every event that she enters.

And, as result, the 2002 Nationals, Olympics, and Worlds promise to be among the most exciting ones ever.

CHAPTER ELEVEN

Hair-Raising Issues

THERE were only a few short weeks between the 2000 U.S. Nationals in February and the 2000 World Championships in March.

So Sarah put her limited time to excellent use.

She worked on her jumps. She worked on her spins. She worked on her placement, her extension, her line, and her carriage.

But, most importantly, she went out, bit the bullet, and she . . . gulp . . . got her hair cut.

To tell the truth, she'd actually wanted to cut it all off the previous year. She'd planned to do it around the same time, right after Nationals and prior to making her World Championship debut. Sarah thought the bun she usually tied her hair up in to skate was too severe. And it sometimes even got caught in her costume. She'd meant to get it cut before last year's Worlds, really she did. But, walking into the shop, getting ready to sit down in the chair and watch the scissors snip away, Sarah got cold feet. Actually, she sort of freaked. Being brave by skating in front of hundreds of thousands of people she could do. But, this—just lopping off your hair like that!—this required serious courage. And so, instead of giving her name to the girl behind the desk and making an appointment, Sarah turned around and walked right out again.

This year though, what with the new millennium and all, Sarah was determined not to chicken out. Why should she? After all, since last year, she'd skated at the World Championships. She'd become a full-time Senior competitor. She'd traveled the world and performed not only in front of judges and fans, but also in front of TV cameras. Why should a girl who'd already faced down all of that with nerves of steel be afraid of a little haircut? Right?

Right?

Nevertheless, as she sat herself down in the stylist's chair, as the apron was tied around her neck and the scissors came closer and closer to her face, Sarah closed her eyes and kept repeating, "If I don't like it, it will grow back. If I don't like it, it will still grow back."

And then she cringed and braced herself.

In just a few short snips, off came the thick hair down to her shoulders. In its place was a short and sassy cut, the edges of which just brushed the back of Sarah's neck. Her new haircut made Sarah's eyes look bigger, and emphasized the warmth of her smile. Plus, "I look more grown-up now," Sarah boasted.

And grown up, very often, was the name of the game in figure skating. In 1995, when it was teenaged Michelle Kwan who was attending her second World Championship, she was a ponytailed little girl wearing no makeup and skating in a dress the color of pink bubble gum. She skated perfectly. She landed everything. It was her best program to date. Michelle was so thrilled, she burst into tears at the end of it. The judges placed her fourth. "Looks too young," they sniffed.

A year later, Michelle Kwan pinned her hair atop her head in a ballerina bun, slathered on black and silver makeup and slipped into a shiny, bare midriff dress. She skated perfectly. She landed everything. Michelle was so thrilled, she burst into tears at the end of it. She became the World Champion.

It was a lesson no skater could afford to miss.

Especially not Sarah Hughes, who, in the qualifying round in Nice, drew to skate in the same group as Michelle, Irina Slutskaya, Viktoria Volchkova, Angela Nikodinov, and the 1997 World bronze medalist from France, Vanessa Gusmeroli. All experienced, polished, and most importantly, mature, skaters.

The qualifying round is an important part of the competition. It's worth a whopping 20 percent of the total score. Skating against the world's best, Sarah finished in third place behind Irina and Michelle.

IFS Editor Lois Elfman was stunned by the improvements she saw in Sarah's skating just a few short weeks after she'd watched her compete at Nationals.

"From the moment she stepped on the ice, she took control of it," Lois recalled. "Sarah had improved every element of her skating. Everything. She and Robin had clearly worked a lot. There was still work to be done, but she definitely seemed like she had made one hundred percent the transition to Senior. Tremendous progress from girl to woman, for sure."

And now, heading into the Short Program, this newly confident young woman would be skating in the World Championship final group of six. This time, Michelle Kwan would be skating first. Sarah drew the fifth slot. Smack dab between Russia's revitalized Irina Slutskaya and veteran Maria Butyrskaya, the defending world champion.

Robin jokingly called Sarah a caviar sandwich.

Caviar because it was a Russian food and Sarah was stuck between two Russians. And also caviar because it was very special. And so was Sarah.

It was the best slot Sarah could have hoped for, skating second to last, and, honestly, much more than she'd ever expected.

And now, since the Ladies' Short Program was scheduled for two days after the qualifying round, she had a whole forty-plus hours to think and worry about it.

To make sure that didn't happen however, Robin insisted that she and Sarah stick to their traditional skating competition routine.

They'd practice, yes, but they would also go out and take a walk, maybe do some shopping, take in a museum or something else educational, then finish up some homework. Anything to keep Sarah from thinking and obsessing about skating.

During their downtime, Sarah and Robin visited the historic old town section of Nice. They would have accompanied Amy Hughes, David, Matt and Taylor on their day trip to Northern Italy, too, but Sarah had a practice session that day. So that she wouldn't feel alone, her dad stayed in Nice to keep Sarah company. Not that he didn't get to see some pretty views, too. The practice rink in Nice had one open side, with a huge window looking out on the hills and palm trees of Monte Carlo. It may have not been Italy, like the rest of the Hughes' were enjoying, but, hey, at least it was something.

And then, before they knew it, it was the night of the Ladies' Short Program. The night for Sarah to stake her claim on a World Championship medal. She would be doing it in a new Short Program dress, a sleeveless beige creation by Tania Bass that some people called "sand" and some called "skin-tone," with a flower pattern and rhinestones.

Her first jump was a double axel, followed almost immediately by a flying camel spin.

"Nice, steady position," praised Dick Button. "Look at how it switches to a forward inside edge."

Next came the most important element of the Short Program—the combination jump. Sarah, like most of the top women, chose to do a triple lutz-double loop. The lutz was the jump Sarah was criticized about most often. Some experts thought she lifted her free leg too high and cheated her entry into the jump by changing her edge at the last minute, in effect doing a flip instead of a lutz.

But, this time around, Dick Button was moved to observe, "This [triple lutz attempt] was much gentler, much straighter and much easier. A good jump combination."

Sarah was halfway home. All that was left was her triple flip, her combination spin, and her spiral combination.

"Excellent extension," Dick Button said about the spiral. Obviously, all of Robin's hard work and encouragement about feeling beautiful and floating on the music had paid off.

And finally, there was the layback spin.

There. Done. Bravo!

"There is a natural elegance to her skating," said Peggy Fleming, as an ecstatic Sarah clapped her hands with delight and took her bows. Then, Sarah skated off the ice and into the kiss and cry area. Exhausted but thrilled with her performance, she sat down next to Robin and waited for her marks.

One of the nine judges gave Sarah a 5.5 for technical elements. Two other judges gave her a 5.0. The rest were all 5.4s with a 5.2 thrown in.

A very broad spread. But Sarah was used to it by now.

"I spun fast, I jumped high, that's all I can ask," Sarah shrugged to *Newsday*. "It's better than a year ago, when I skated the best I could in the Short and wound up ninth."

It certainly was better.

At the end of the Short Program, at her second World Championship, Sarah Hughes was sitting in fourth place behind defending champion Maria Butyrskaya, Irina Slut-skaya, and Michelle Kwan.

She was definitely a medal contender.

She was also the youngest skater at the competition. Not only among the ladies, but, among the pairs, dancers, and men, too. To some, it may have seemed like the word "youngest" didn't really belong in the same sentence as contender.

But, Sarah believes anything is possible. She is, after all, a self-described optimist. And she knows that the key trick to not getting intimidated by skating with the best in the world is just to remember what had gotten her there: a lot of work, dedication, and the belief that she could do it.

If those three things had gotten her to Worlds, wasn't it logical then that they could also take her to the medal podium?

UNFORTUNATELY for Sarah though, for the second year in a row, a medal just wasn't in the cards.

Even though Sarah skated well overall, she had slight mistakes on the landings of both her triple-triple combinations, even having to touch the ice with her hand once to keep from falling.

Maybe it was because of all the waiting. Sarah skated last in the competition.

When she realized she'd drawn the twenty-fourth spot, only two words ran through her head.

"Oh, no!"

She also had to skate in the same warm-up group as crowd favorite Michelle Kwan. As Sarah confessed to *International Figure Skating Magazine*, "During the warm-up, the audience was chanting, 'Go, Michelle!' pretty loudly. But, that didn't really bother me. All I was thinking about was my skating. As a skater, I have to be prepared to skate under any circumstances."

Yet, even though she stayed focused and together, Sarah's flawed routine dropped her from fourth place down into fifth. Two spots out of the medals. And yet, unlike the thirteen-year-old who'd been disappointed with a pewter medal at her very first Senior Nationals, she was still pleased. At the end of her long program, Sarah felt she had given it all she had. Even if, as Robin suspected, a part of Sarah, despite being pleased with her overall performance through all three rounds of the competition, was still dwelling on the wobbled triple-triple combinations.

To those who congratulated her, praising Sarah for her achievement—only fourteen years old and fifth in the World!—Sarah offered a polite and gracious thank-you, but she also quickly added that she hadn't been thinking about placings. She was just happy with what she did, and the overall feelings she came away with.

"I wasn't intimidated by the others," Sarah told *Newsday*. "I've always wanted to skate against the best. I was proud of myself. A lot of these women have been here many, many times before, and it's only my second time at Worlds. Fifth is more than I can ask for. My goal was to move up from last year, and I moved up two spots. I can't be disappointed."

Robin added, "I won't say any of this has been surprising, but, of course, we are thoroughly pleased. We've been very, very careful to set goals that were within her dreams, but yet were very much reasonable. The goals we set are not defined in terms of specific placements at certain events, but rather goals that relate to how she performs and what we get out of each competitive season. At no time have we pressed too hard or expected too much. She's just been able to raise the bar each year."

Not that either Sarah or Robin were naive about how much more she still had left to accomplish and work on.

Fortunately, Sarah describes herself as very self-motivated. She and Robin both believed, in 2000, that Sarah was capable of a lot more. Pushing and pushing for improvement was what had gotten her as far as she already was, and it would be the key thing that would take her further. Even before she left Nice, Sarah was already talking about her plans for next year.

Her goals were simple, clear, and direct. Next year, Sarah wanted to be on the podium at Nationals. And at Worlds.

And, in two years, Sarah intended to be at the Olympics.

To that end, Sarah and Robin decided that the Summer of 2000 would be the most intense one they'd ever trained. Not only would they continue their efforts to improve Sarah's unsteady lutz, her spins, her presentation, her overall look, they also decided that, this summer, they would start working on her triple axel jump.

The triple axel is the most difficult jump a woman has ever landed in competition. Japan's Midori Ito landed one at the 1989 Worlds, and made history. America's Tonya Harding became the first American woman to land one both at the 1991 U.S. Nationals and the 1991 World Championship. Since then, Russia's Maria Butyrskaya has landed some in practice, and, periodically, there are reports of other girls in other rinks supposedly landing them as well. But a jump is only ratified if it's landed in competition. And no American lady had done one in ten years.

Naturally, Sarah, the little girl who'd taught herself to tie her own skates, was itching to give it a shot. She figured, if she was going to make a mark on the world scene in this critical, pre-Olympic season, a triple axel would be a pretty good way to make sure everyone knew that Sarah Hughes had arrived and was ready to do battle.

The first day of her new summer training regiment, Sarah was psyched to try that triple axel. But, first, she needed to warm up. Do some easy single and double jumps. Do some spins, do some basic stroking. The usual routine.

And it was while stroking, while skating backward at top speed, that Sarah crashed into the boards. *Bam!*

She put out her hand to protect herself and instantly felt a burning, stabbing pain radiating up through her palm, into her wrist, up her entire arm.

Sarah cried out, falling. Robin was immediately by her side, realizing that this wasn't just a simple fall. This could be serious.

She and Sarah hurried to the hospital, trying to protect her throbbing arm the best they could from being jostled in the car ride on the way over.

There, the doctors offered Sarah what they thought was a pretty good diagnosis. Her hand was broken, yes. But, the break wasn't too complex; all Sarah needed was six weeks in a cast, and she'd be as good as new.

Six weeks may not have seemed like a long time to a doctor used to putting his patients to bed for years at a time. But, for an up-and-coming skater who knew she didn't have a moment to waste, six weeks was an eternity.

No, it was worse than an eternity. It was a death sentence. In all of her life, starting from the age of three, Sarah Hughes had never, ever spent six weeks off the ice.

Her immediate reaction was disbelief—how could she have hurt herself not by jumping, not by spinning, but simply by skating backward? How stupid was that?

Followed by depression.

The girl who once explained to a reporter, "The one thing I couldn't live without is my skating!" was now hearing that she wouldn't be able to do it for almost two months.

Robin and the rest of the Hugheses tried to keep Sarah's spirits up. They suggested that, to keep in shape while she recuperated, Sarah take up some aerobic training like running, walking, and biking.

Sarah leaped on the suggestion like a drowning swimmer grasping for a life preserver. And, like everything else in her life, she tackled her new project with 100 percent tenacity.

Sarah's dad thought that Sarah was just like her mother in that way. He told the *New York Times*, "Amy's got a spirit you just can't slow down. Sarah got that spirit from her, a real drive that gets her to train as hard as she does."

Unfortunately, during the summer of 2000, that drive proved to be a bit much. Within a few days of throwing herself into aerobic training, Sarah strained her hip muscle.

Wonderful.

Now, she couldn't do anything at all!

If Sarah thought she was depressed before, that wasn't anything compared to how rotten she felt now.

Unable to skate, unable to run or train in any other way, there was nothing left for the fifteen-year-old to do but sit around, wallowing in her unhappiness.

Without a daily training regiment, Sarah started to put on weight. In addition, she'd grown almost two inches, now measuring five feet, four and a half inches. Pretty tall for a competitive skater. Tonya Harding, who'd landed the last American triple axel, stood only a little more than five feet tall. Midori Ito was barely four feet nine inches. Would Sarah's extra height and weight—almost a totally brand-new body, really—keep her from joining them in the history books?

"I was sort of depressed," Sarah told the *New York Times*.

"I got out of shape, I wasn't training really, and I sort of got off track."

Robin added, "She was down in the dumps, her body wasn't in the shape she wanted it to be and we were nearing the competitive season. I knew she wasn't emotionally and physically ready for it. There were a lot of tears, and it was a big growing up time for her."

Which meant that it was time for Robin to intervene.

Even though, under normal circumstances, Robin described her star pupil with the compliment, "She's a very well-rounded kid. She's a regular kid. She's a funny kid. She likes to goof around," Robin knew that now was not the time for the two of them to be goofing. It wasn't time to be talking about those new shoes that Sarah wanted to get or the CD she wanted to play at the rink. It was time to get serious.

Getting serious meant making an appointment with a nutritionist, who put Sarah on a new, healthy diet. It also meant teaching Sarah to ignore the whispers that were springing up in the skating world, mostly on the Internet message boards that Robin doesn't allow Sarah to read or even go out, that last year's U.S. bronze medalist might not be ready for the upcoming season. That she was probably on the way out.

Robin told Sarah it was time to fight. It was time to prove that Sarah Hughes had what it takes to stand on the podium at Worlds and Olympics. It was time for Sarah to prove it to the public.

And to herself.

CHAPTER TWELVE

Fighting Back

A newly grown-up Sarah took the ice for the 2000–2001 season.

She wasn't grown up because of her new layered haircut, or because of her growth spurt, or because her costumes for the season featured more skin and plunging necklines. She was grown up because she'd spent the summer feeling down on herself, on skating, on basically, the whole world.

But, now she was back. She was ready to fight and challenge and persevere. Not like a little girl anymore, but like a woman.

The difference was obvious starting with her first Grand Prix event, Skate America. The event where, in the fall of 2000, Sarah Hughes came a lot closer to beating Michelle Kwan than she ever had before. She ended up placing second, but many whispered that, with her perfect skate, she should have gotten the gold.

Next came the Cup of Russia, where Sarah finished third behind reigning Grand Prix champion Irina Slutskaya and another hometown favorite, Olympian Elena Sokolova. At the Nations Cup in Germany, she finished second only to 1999 World Champion Maria Butyrskaya.

Three Grand Prix events, three medals. Good enough to qualify for the Grand Prix Final. Where, much to the surprise of practically everyone, the debuting fifteen-year-old won the bronze medal over the same Butyrskaya who'd beaten her only a few weeks earlier.

In the middle of this busy season Sarah also unveiled a new interpretative free and exhibition program to music from the Broadway musical *Fosse*. This was a new Sarah— sexy, sophisticated and sultry. Sarah worked hard on incorporating trademark Fosse dance moves into the program, and getting the attitude just right. It was an immediate hit with audiences everywhere.

"It's probably the best four weeks of my life," Sarah confessed to the Associated Press. "(Going in), people didn't say, 'Oh, well, it's between Michelle Kwan and Sarah Hughes.' My name was never really mentioned. Then to come and surprise everybody as Robin and I did here, it was fun. It was like, 'Hey, I'm here!' "

And it was a heady record with which to head into the 2001 U.S. Nationals in Boston, Massachusetts. A record that had more than a few experts and reporters asking: Can Sarah Hughes upset Michelle Kwan for the title?

"It's wide open," Robin told *The Daily News*. "More than ever, the reality is Michelle is beatable."

"I don't think [Michelle's] a lock," Sarah agreed. "I feel the same way as my coach."

"I hope for her to be on the podium at least in second place, if no higher than that," Robin realistically elaborated for the Associated Press. "I understand you can't just do one performance and necessarily be at the top. It's earning the respect of the judges. I think she's really reached that level now."

IFS editor Lois Elfman agreed. Asked to handicap Sarah's chances, she offered, "Is Sarah Michelle Kwan, yet? No, not in the overall sense. I think Michelle has an ability that's just superb. She doesn't always hit it, but, when she hits, at her best, she's extraordinary. Sarah is not there yet, but I think she can go head to head with Michelle Kwan, because Michelle Kwan isn't always on. If Michelle is her best and Sarah is her best, Michelle will win. But Sarah certainly has all the qualities to compete with her."

Sarah agreed. "It all depends on my skating. I'll get what I deserve. No more."

IN the end, both Robin and Sarah proved prescient.

Sarah Hughes skated well. Not well enough to defeat a less than perfect Kwan, but well enough to win the silver medal. In just three years, she'd moved up from fourth to third to second. It was a very nice and very promising progression. And a very quick one. Even Michelle Kwan was only sixth at her first Senior Nationals, then second twice before winning the title.

Did Sarah's ascent seem particularly fast to her?

"At first, you don't really notice," Sarah admitted to the Associated Press. "I go to the rink every day and it doesn't seem overnight. Then I look back and it's like, wow! The 1999 Nationals were only two years ago. It's crazy!"

But, enough about the past. As soon as Nationals were over and the silver medal hung around her neck, Sarah was busy looking toward the future, and the World Championships in Canada, her dad's home country.

Going into Worlds, Sarah's main goal was to, all three times, come off the ice feeling really good about her performance. After all, how she skated was the only part of the event that was in Sarah's control. The rest was in the hands of the judges.

UNLIKE most competitors, who spend their free weeks between Nationals and Worlds working extra hard, Sarah actually took a week off from skating to rest.

"I can't be so intense all the time," Sarah told iskater. com. "At events there's a lot of extra pressure and mental stuff so you have to take some come downtime."

Pretty mellow words for a girl generally so intense that her clothes closet at home is arranged by season, color, and sleeve length.

But the Sarah who came to the Worlds in Canada was a lot less perfection-oriented then she had been in the past.

Her summer spent off the ice had taught Sarah a lot of valuable lessons.

"I think I learned about life," she confessed to the *New York Times*. "That things don't always go as planned."

And yet, for a young woman who wasn't going to be so obsessive anymore, the 2001 Worlds seemed to go pretty close to plan.

To start matters off on the right foot, Sarah finished second in her qualifying round, behind Michelle Kwan and ahead of Angela Nikodinov and Maria Butyrskaya. (This despite Robin grousing that a qualifying round made it tough for the skaters to pace themselves, and that she wished they didn't have to skate it.)

Next came a critical phase of the competition—the Short Program, worth 30 percent of the score. Conventional wisdom says a skater can't win a competition in the Short Program, but they definitely can lose it here. Sarah was skating her short to Sergei Rochmaninoff's *Vocalise*, and the program really emphasized her grace, flow and mature elegance. The idea behind the program was Sarah's relationship to the ice, so at the beginning and end of the program Sarah touches the ice with her hand to convey this idea.

In the Short Program, as Sarah told *International Figure Skating*, "I felt trained and ready for competition, but during the Short I was very nervous and my legs were shaking!"

Nevertheless, Sarah did manage to keep both Maria and Viktoria Volchkova at bay, even though American teammate Angela Nikodinov slipped into third place behind Irina and Michelle, and Sarah dropped down to fourth.

It was the same spot she'd sat in last year.

Last year, when she'd let a medal slip through her fingers.

Would history repeat itself?

Only the Long Program would tell.

"REPRESENTING the United States of America—Sarah Hughes!"

Sarah stepped out onto the ice. She glided to the center.

She smiled confidently and saucily tossed her head to get into character. Her music began. The first notes of *Don Quixote* floated across the filled-to-capacity arena.

"Pa-ra-pa-rum-pum-pum-pum-PUM-PUM!"

Sarah didn't move.

"Sarah's coach," Peggy Fleming told the television audience, "has said that this program is more demanding emotionally this year, because they are trying to have her portray the character of *Don Quixote* and perform a dance."

"Pa-ra-pa-rum-pum-pum-pum-PUM-PUM!"

Sarah still didn't move.

"Pa-ra-pa-rum-PUM!"

Finally, finally! She took her first step.

And within a few moments exploded into a double axel.

Perfect.

After that it was time for the triple salchow-triple loop. Clean and landed.

"This is what makes this program so technically difficult," Peggy explained.

Combination spin. Triple loop.

The music built to a crescendo as Sarah skidded to a stop right in front of the judges. She smiled, she rolled her shoulders, and, as her music grew more saucy and sexy, Sarah flirted with the entire judging panel in perfect character to her Spanish-themed music.

A triple lutz-double toe. A spiral now, with one hand planted on her hip, to make it more difficult. She spiraled forward, she spiraled backward. The crowd applauded enthusiastically.

Triple flip. Flying camel. And now a bouncy, jaunty footwork sequence so full of life and energy that the entire audience clapped along with the music to show their approval.

Sarah went into a layback spin. The one maneuver Dick Button and Peggy Fleming agree has been the weakest among the recent American ladies.

And yet, as Sarah spun, Peggy was moved to gush, "This layback spin is absolutely perfect position. Good arch in the back and a beautiful free leg and turned out foot."

One more triple lutz landed!

She was three-quarters of the way home now, and, to celebrate, Sarah flung her hands triumphantly in the air.

Triple toe. Also perfect.

"Is she a competitor!" Peggy exclaimed.

Finally, a combination spin. The crowd began clapping even before she'd finished. In Canada, where thousands of spectators come to the World Championship just to watch practices, they knew a star-making turn when they saw one.

And so did Sarah Hughes.

As she finished her program perfectly in time with the music, she pumped her fist with glee and, carried away, gave herself a well-deserved hand before remembering where she was, and quickly composing herself to formally take her bows.

Sarah had kept her promise to herself. After three phases of the competition, she felt good about how she'd skated.

"I had to grab the chance to put it over," she told *The Great Neck Record*, later. "If I stayed safe, I wouldn't have even been noticed."

In Kiss-and-Cry, Sarah sat with Robin and waited for her marks to come up on the scoreboard.

The technicals were flashed first. Sarah Hughes' marks ranged from 5.3 from one judge to three 5.7s and even a 5.8.

And now the presentation marks.

Sarah and Robin held their breaths.

This was critical. This was their chance to see if the judges had really noticed Sarah's improvement over the last year. They'd worked so hard on it. *IFS* editor Lois Elfman, for one, thought that Sarah had made remarkable progress in that area.

"The elements that go into the presentation mark are,"

she counted off each one, "Variation of speed, which Sarah had. Utilization of the ice surface, she's excellent at that—she doesn't seem to just do her program in one spot, she knows how to work the entire ice. Easy movement and sureness. She has that. Carriage and style. Sarah has good carriage, she has wonderful posture. Originality. A nice selection of music, she certainly tried to bring it to life. Expression of the character of the music, that was very strong. Now, did she do *Don Quixote* like (the great Russian ballerina) Natalia Makarova? No. But it was obvious from her choreography that someone had shown her what the whole mood of the music was. It was definitely right up there."

As if to confirm such a positive assessment, Sarah's presentation scores ranged from two 5.5s to three 5.8s. The girl who everyone once wrote off as more of a jumper than an artist had just received higher scores for her presentation that she did for her technical!

Good enough to win the bronze medal!

Sarah and Robin both screamed with delight when they found out, and fell, joyful, into each other's arms.

Nevertheless, an ecstatic and giddy Sarah wasn't so overwhelmed that she forgot exactly whom she owed her triumph to. She gushed to *International Figure Skating*, "Robin's extra energy is what got me on the podium this year. She and I both feel like I have more inside me to bring out. I just need to work hard, meet the challenges before me, and get more experience. There is always more to aspire to. I want to keep impressing people, keep getting faster, stronger, pushing the envelope."

Less than a year before the 2002 Olympics, Sarah Hughes had, quite unconsciously, spelled out her goals for the future using some of the same words as the Olympic credo.

Swifter. Higher. Stronger.

Salt Lake City, here she comes!

The Future

So what's next for Sarah Hughes?

The answer may be a simple numbers game.

After finishing fourth, then third, then second at Nationals, and seventh, then fifth, then third at Worlds, what else could possibly be left for Sarah but a number one spot atop both podiums?

And what about the Olympics? Sarah Hughes has no record at the Olympics, and yet the numbers suggest that she will be representing the United States come February of 2002.

With the whole world watching, does Sarah Hughes have a chance to win a medal in Salt Lake City? Absolutely!

Again, it's a numbers game, a game of statistics, probabilities and historical precedent. In 1998, the three women on the podium, America's Tara Lipinski and Michelle Kwan, and China's Lu Chen had all won medals at previous World Championships. The same was true for two 1994 medalists, Ukraine's Oksana Baiul and America's Nancy Kerrigan; three 1992 medalists, America's Kristi Yamaguchi, Japan's Midori Ito and Nancy Kerrigan; and two 1988 medalists, East Germany's Katarina Witt and America's Debi Thomas. As the defending World bronze medalist, Sarah Hughes will definitely be one to watch in Salt Lake City.

And winning a medal at the Olympics is very different from winning a medal, any medal of any color, at the World Championships. When you win a medal at the World Championships, your name becomes known to a relatively small group of devoted skating fans. But, when you win a medal at the Olympics, the whole world suddenly knows your name! As USOlympicTeam.com wrote in February of 2001, "[Sarah Hughes] could be twelve months away from having the better part of a nation fall in love with her."

In other words, Sarah will be famous. Not just a little bit famous like she is now, but very, very famous. There will be even more interviews, more television crews and reporters showing up at school, more live performances, more shows, more specials, tours, autographs.

It's tempting to wonder: If Sarah becomes a major sports star, what kind of effect will it have on the more or less normal life she currently has? Will she still be able to act like a regular kid back in her history class? Will she still be able to get her hair cut at the mall? Will her brothers and sisters get jealous of all the attention?

Based on what's happened so far, the answer to that last question seems to be: probably not. Right now, Sarah's brothers and sisters aren't jealous of Sarah's fame because they all have their own lives to worry about. Rebecca is a Harvard University graduate who recently got married. David and Matt play college and high school hockey, and besides, as Sarah told *Newsday*, "My brothers aren't jealous. They're happy to (travel) with me when I'm around all these women."

And for the younger girls, Emily and Taylor, there are fringe benefits to having a skating star sister, too. Whenever Sarah skates a particularly good performance, fans shower her with teddy bears and other toys, which they throw on the ice. Sarah always collects all of her gifts and makes sure to read the letters people attach to them. But, obviously, she can't keep them all. So, Emily and Taylor get to pick out some favorites for their own collections. The ones that are left over, Sarah and her mom donate to local children's hospitals so that sick kids can have something soft to cuddle when they get scared or lonely.

And who knows, it might not be long before the littlest Hughes are being showered with teddy bears of their own. Emily, after all, is a competitive skater, too. She's already qualified once for the Junior Olympics. And Taylor, well, she's the really talented one. Taylor does both figure skating and hockey!

As her dad has said, "Taylor is keeping her options open."

In fact, about the only Hughes family member who

doesn't have his own skating career is the clan's dog, a golden retriever named Sport.

"He was on the ice once," Amy Hughes told *The Great Neck Record*, "And had to be slid off."

So it's likely that even Sport won't be too jealous if Sarah wins a medal in Salt Lake City.

Or in Turin, Italy, in 2006.

Because, the fact is, unlike some of the older competitors, like Russia's Maria Butyrskaya or even Michelle Kwan, it's highly likely that 2002 will not be Sarah's last Olympic Games.

As Lois Elfman points out, "Sarah showed progress every year. She progressed at a good pace, as opposed to something shot out of a cannon, which is what's going to give her great longevity. She's a good performer. I think she can continue to compete certainly until the 2006 Olympics."

The question is, will she want to? Unlike many skaters who can't imagine a life off the ice, Sarah has other professional ambitions. Although she used to want to be a lawyer like her father, ever since her mother's illness and recovery Sarah has been leaning more toward a medical career. She's admitted to really admiring the doctors who treated her mom, and thinks she might like to go into the research field and find a cure for diseases.

If Sarah does decide to hang up her skates for a stethoscope, she'll be in good company. 1956 Olympic Champion and five-time U.S. Champion Tenley Albright is a doctor. So is 1987 World Champion and two-time U.S. Champion Debi Thomas.

But let's not get ahead of ourselves. All of the big professional decisions—both on and off the ice—are still far in the future. Sarah, after all, despite being a seasoned international competitor, will only be sixteen years old in Salt Lake City.

Even if she is one sixteen-year-old who would do well to brush up on the words to "The Star Spangled Banner"—just in case she might be called upon to sing it someday soon.

"If that moment comes," Sarah has said, "I'll have so many different thoughts going through my head. But, I bet I could sing it."

And, come February of 2002, she may very well get to.

PROFILE

BORN: May 2, 1985

HOME CLUB: Skating Club of New York

HOMETOWN: Great Neck, NY

TRAINS: The Ice House, Hackensack, NJ

SCHOOL: Great Neck North High School

COACH/CHOREOGRAPHER: Robin Wagner

SARAH HUGHES'S COMPETITIVE RECORD

2001 Great American Figure Skating Challenge (Team) 3rd

2001 World Championships—3rd

2001 Grand Prix Final—3rd

2001 U.S. Championships—2nd

2000 Canadian Open—3rd

2000 Hershey's Kisses Challenge (Team)-1st

2000 Cup of Russia—3rd

2000 Nations Cup—2nd

2000 Skate America—2nd

2000 Int. Figure Skating Challenge (Team)—2nd

2000 World Championships—5th

2000 U.S. Figure Skating Championships—3rd
1999 Keri Lotion USA vs. World (Team)—1st
1999 Trophee Lalique—3rd
1999 Skate America—4th
1999 Vienna Cup—1st
1999 Keri Lotion Classic (Team USA)—2nd
1999 Hershey's Kisses (Team USA)—2nd
1999 World Championships—7th
1999 ISU Junior Grand Prix—2nd
1999 U.S. Championships—4th
1999 World Junior Championships—2nd
1998 Hungarian Trophy—2nd
1999 World Junior Team Selection—1st
1998 Mexico Cup—2nd
1998 U.S. Junior Championships—1st
1998 Eastern Junior—1st
1998 North Atlantic Junior—1st
1997 Eastern Novice—6th
1997 North Atlantic Novice—1st
1996 Eastern Novice—10th
1996 North Atlantic Novice—3rd

FOR MORE INFORMATION ABOUT SARAH HUGHES,
CHECK OUT THE FOLLOWING WEBSITES:

The Unofficial Sarah Hughes Page at:
    www.dianesrink.com/sarah/

Sarah Hughes: Skater for the New Millennium at:
    www.geocities.com/Wellesley/Garden/6716/

Sarah Hughes: Pure Talent at:
   www.geocities.com/mvsarah/

Sarah Hughes: Grace on Ice at:
   www.geocities.com/sarahhughes2002/